CW01467932

# THE VICTORIAN SCHOOLDAY

## A TEACHER'S MANUAL

**Wynne Frankum**
*Katesgrove Schoolroom*

**Jo Lawrie**
*Sevington School*

# CONTENTS

PROLOGUE — Page 4

INTRODUCTION — Page 6

PLANNING A VICTORIAN SCHOOLDAY — Page 7

THE VICTORIAN SCHOOLROOM — Page 8
EQUIPMENT — Page 10
ACTIVITIES BEFORE THE DAY — Page 11
DRESS — Page 12
TAKING ON ANOTHER ROLE — Page 16
VICTORIAN BEHAVIOUR — Page 17
- The Pupils — Page 17
- School Rules — Page 19
- The Teacher — Page 20
THE TIMETABLE — Page 22

ORGANISING THE DAY — Page 25

THE REGISTER — Page 25
THE COLLECTION OF SCHOOL PENNIES — Page 25
INSPECTION — Page 25
PRAYERS — Page 26
HYMNS — Page 27
BIBLE READING AND MORAL HOMILY — Page 29
THE LESSONS — Page 30
- Reading — Page 30
- Writing, Dictation and Spelling — Page 32
- Tables — Page 34
- Arithmetic — Page 34
- Religious Instruction — Page 36
- Drill — Page 38
- History — Page 40
- Geography — Page 45
- The Object Lesson — Page 49
- Science — Page 50
- Drawing — Page 51
- Sewing — Page 52
- A Moral Tale — Page 55
- Singing — Page 55
- Vocal Gymnastics — Page 56
- Poetry — Page 57
A VISIT BY THE INSPECTOR — Page 60
PRESENTATION OF CERTIFICATES & MEDALS — Page 61
AN EVENING PRAYER — Page 62

APPENDICES                                                    Page 63

   I      EDUCATION 1762 - 1902                          Page 64
         (an outline for the teacher)

   II     MAJOR EVENTS 1810 - 1901                       Page 65
         (for a class time-line)

   III    VICTORIAN CHILDREN'S NAMES                     Page 65

   IV    FOLLOW-UP WORK                                 Page 66

            - Discussion                            Page 66

            - Art and Craft                         Page 66

            - Cooking                               Page 66

            - Games and Rhymes                       Page 67

   V      A SAMPLE COPYBOOK FOR REPRODUCING              Page 68

   VI     BIBLIOGRAPHY                                   Page 71

   VII    VICTORIAN SCHOOLS, SCHOOL MUSEUMS
         & MUSEUMS OF CHILDHOOD                         Page 71

   VIII  SUPPLIERS                                      Page 72

## LIST OF CONTENTS IN *THE VICTORIAN SCHOOLDAY* RESOURCE FOLDER *

1.  Outline of Union Jack
2.  Family tree of Queen Victoria
3.  1837 - 'Your Majesty is Queen of England'
4.  Queen Victoria as an elderly widow
5.  A map of the Empire
6.  A moral tract
7.  Bible print - Noah's Ark
8.  Bible print - The Calming of the Waves
9.  Infant Reading chart
10. Alphabet chart
11. Pattern for girl's pinafore
12. Patterns for boys' collars

* *A collection of A3 resource material which may be purchased from Katesgrove Schoolroom or Sevington School either separately or to accompany this teacher's manual.*

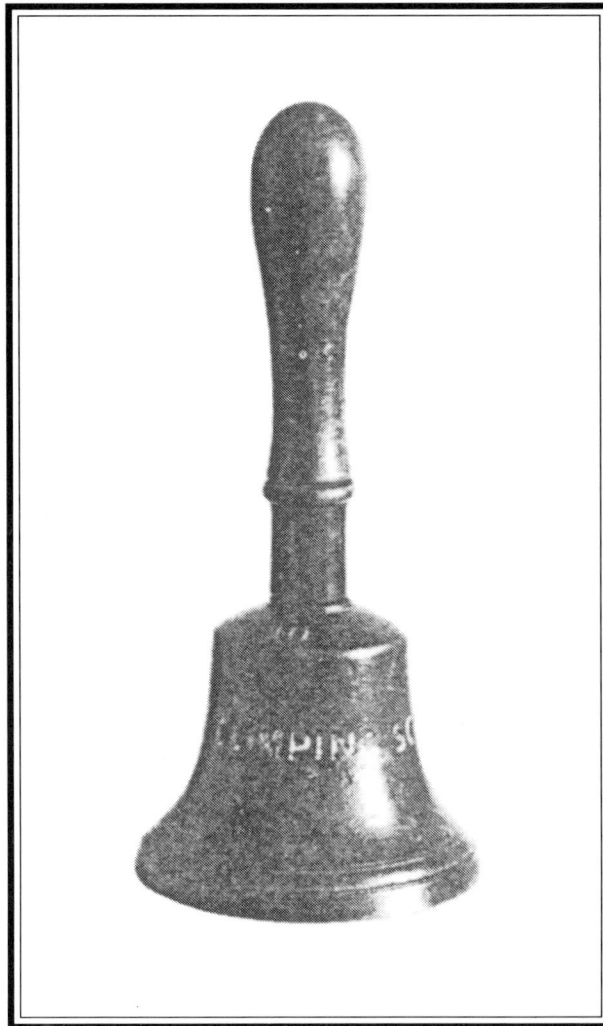

## PROLOGUE

This 'TEACHER'S MANUAL' seeks to help you to plan a realistic Victorian schoolday.

It can be referred to by teachers converting their own classroom or by those visiting one of the schoolrooms listed in Appendix VII.

The manual is based on careful research and on personal experience of many of the pitfalls involved in striving for authenticity.

It is intended to encourage historical work of quality and depth and to foster an understanding of the past.

Because this is a reference book it is quite detailed, therefore it is anticipated that users will be selective.

# INTRODUCTION

A visit to a Victorian classroom can be integrated into the history content of the national curriculum as part of CSU3, Victorian Britain or as part of Supplementary Study Unit B, Local History.

(It could also meet the requirements of the national curriculum drama document or be part of a cross-curricular approach. You might compare a ground plan of your school with that of a Victorian one, also looking at the plumbing, heating and lighting.)

It is important to ensure that the following elements are included:

1. A SENSE OF CHRONOLOGY e.g. time-lines starting with the child and its family can give information about both the Victorian era and educational change.

2. A BACKGROUND KNOWLEDGE OF EVERYDAY LIFE to include homes, clothes, diet, shops, jobs, transport, entertainment etc.

3. VARIED SOURCES OF EVIDENCE e.g. pictures and old photographs; artefacts; documents, such as school registers and logbooks; oral history; visits to places of interest; computer based material.

4. LINKS WITH ATTAINMENT TARGETS e.g. 'then and now', comparing the Victorian classroom with the modern classroom; discussing the comparative reliability of different types of evidence.

5. INDEPENDENT WORK BY PUPILS who should learn to investigate, organise and communicate the results of their own historical knowledge and understanding in a variety of ways.

6. AUTHENTICITY in the Victorian classroom which can be reflected in the furniture; the artefacts; the decoration of the walls; the costume; the role play of teacher and pupil; the organisation of the day and the content of the lessons.

## PLANNING A VICTORIAN SCHOOLDAY

Attention to detail is vital if children are to be provided with a suitable
historical context for the sort of valuable first hand experience recommended
in the national curriculum history document.  The preparations for the
Victorian schoolday should involve pupils in personal research and can be
used as a focus for attainment targets e.g. comparing clothes then and now.
To gain full benefit from the exercise, one school converted a room into
a Victorian classroom for a week and each class spent a day in there.
Equally, if you are going to the expense and trouble of hiring a coach to
go to an existing schoolroom, it is worth maximising the value of the visit
by ensuring that everything is as authentic as possible.

## THE VICTORIAN SCHOOLROOM

An original or reconstructed classroom (as at Sevington or Katesgrove, see Appendix VII) is the ideal but you can also transform your own classroom, even if it is modern. You might even use the school hall for a large group.

The room should be made to look bare, so it may be necessary to take down or to cover up most of the children's work. Twentieth century equipment which is not required can be either removed or screened off with a curtain or a roll of corrugated paper. If there are 2 entrances to the room they could have notices above and outside so that one is for boys and the other for girls.

Suitable decorations might include a picture of Queen Victoria, a Union Jack, a map of the Empire, a religious picture or a moral tract.

Artefacts, which need not be original, could include a sampler, an abacus, an ink bottle, slates, copybooks and a dunce's cap (or 'fool's cap' as it is referred to in Garlick's 'New Manual of Method'). An old-fashioned vase of flowers and a pile of old books would be effective 'props'.

The windows can be altered by making high, 'gothic' type frames out of black paper. (Windows were set high up to help with the diffusion of light and to avoid draughts and damage.) Try to use natural light and only turn on the electric lights if it is a particularly gloomy day. If possible the pupils should sit with the windows on their left so that their right hand does not cast a shadow when they are writing.

Desks must be in rows facing the teacher's desk and the blackboard. A blackboard and easel is most authentic but a wall-mounted or roller board would do. If a blackboard is not available, large sheets of black paper can be fixed to the wall.

Victorian elementary schools were divided into standards, starting with Standard I at 7 years. Pupils' ability was tested annually by the school inspector. Normally, children could expect to move up one standard each year, reaching Standard VII by the age of thirteen or fourteen. However, pupils who did not pass the exam stayed put; whereas a bright child could jump several standards. In practice, it meant that there could be an eleven year old in Standard I and an eight year old in Standard V. (If you have pupils in your class above the age of 11, some could have reached Standard VI or VII but many children left school at 13 without getting beyond Standard V.)

In a large school there would have been a separate classroom for the children in each standard. However, if there were just one large schoolroom or if it were a small school all the children from different standards would have been taught in the same room. Even with a head teacher, a teacher and a pupil teacher the organisation of such a class could present problems.

The present day teacher, planning a Victorian schoolday, may find it most convenient to pretend that all the class has reached a particular standard. However, if the pupils are from a small, rural school with a variety of ages it might be necessary to have pupils of different standards doing different work at the same time.

If children are in the same standard they should be seated alphabetically or in order of age or size. If they are in different standards they should be seated with Standard I at the front and Standard V at the rear. Boys and girls sit separately, with girls to the left of the boys i.e. on the right side of the room from the teacher's vantage point.

Monitors may be selected to give out books, slates etc. and they can be positioned at the end of the row, for convenience. Choose plenty of monitors so that a good number of pupils get a chance to move about and be involved.

· VILLAGE · SCHOOL · HOUSE ·

· ERECTED · AT · HULLAVINGTON · WILTS · 1832.

BY JOSEPH NEELD ESQ.RE M.P.

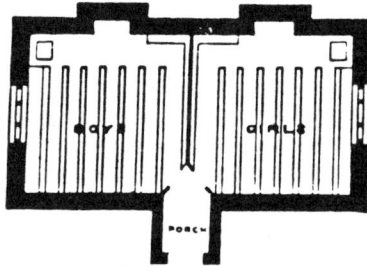

*This scrappy note in the front of the Sevington School register of 1886 gives us the sort of detail that is not normally recorded and therefore difficult to acquire. [a simple illustration that 12d = 1/– (one shilling).]*

9

## EQUIPMENT

*All items should be made out of natural rather than synthetic materials.*

Teacher's desk at the front, preferably raised.

King James Bible and a Prayer Book.

A register and an attendance board.

Pupils' desks in rows facing the front.

Blackboard and pointer (a piece about 50 cm/20 ins long, cut from a cane).

A school bell and a metal whistle.

Victorian pennies to pay school fees.

Sand trays, for the infants, can be made from shoe box lids.

Slates can be bought (see Appendix VIII for suppliers) or made out of black paper or card.

Slate pencils were used originally but chalk may have to be substituted.

(N.B. If you are using slate pencils you may be interested to note that they were sharpened against the outside wall of the school. Some older schools have evidence of this i.e. grooves worn into the stone or brickwork near the entrances. Ludlow Middle School, Southampton, still has a special hard stone inset in the outside wall which was intended for sharpening slate pencils).

Small pieces of real sponge or flannel cloth (or similar absorbent material) for cleaning the slates. Modern synthetic fabric is neither authentic nor effective.

Copybooks can be made from the photocopiable material in Appendix V.

Lead pencils were expensive and often did not appear in village schools until the end of the 19th century. Even then they were used for drawing rather than writing.

Writing materials i.e. dip-in pens, ink, pen wipers (circles of felt or absorbent material such as flannel sewn together in the middle) and blotting paper. (If ink wells are not available small Indian ink bottles with ordinary black ink are most suitable. You might consider using a washable blue/black ink instead of the more authentic black although that washes out with biological powder.)

Wax crayons and drawing paper.

Reproduction Victorian reading books can be bought (see Appendix VIII).

Sewing materials i.e. pieces of calico, coloured thread (so that the stitches show up clearly), extra short needles, metal thimbles and scissors without plastic handles.

Large wooden beads and shoe laces for threading, by the infants.

Objects for the object lesson and plants for drawing.

Dunce's cap and the cane (a thin garden cane, which is both flexible and strong).

Reproduction Victorian toys such as wooden building bricks, cup and ball, marbles, wooden skittles, hoops, whip and top, skipping ropes and diabolo could be provided for playtime.

## ACTIVITIES BEFORE THE DAY

There is specific work which could usefully be done in advance of the Victorian schoolday. Obviously, this would be according to the age and ability of the children.

1.  Learning imperial measurement.

2.  Familiarity with pounds, shillings and pence.

3.  Handwriting practice using the copybook.

4.  Practising tables and any appropriate rhymes, prayers or songs.

5.  Discussion of suitable behaviour in the classroom.

6.  If possible get both the adults and the children to wear Victorian dress beforehand. This gives a chance to make any tactful requests to change obvious anachronisms.

7.  Children can choose Victorian names if their own are too modern. Practise using them and   adjust the register accordingly.  Some classes have used their 'Victorian' register for a  week or so before the visit to familiarise everyone with the new names.  If pupils are to wear a label it would be better to have a Victorian-looking one which they have made out of card rather than a modern stick-on label.

8.  Pupils should be warned that the teachers will be much stricter than they are normally and that this is because they are in role.

9.  Practising role-play in advance can help to eradicate any self-consciousness or giggling. Also the children need to know details of each others' 'lives' e.g. size of family, their fathers' jobs etc. Pupils need sufficient background knowledge to ensure that the content of their role-play is authentic e.g. they would not have known about anything which has been invented since the 19th century.

10.  In a class with pupils from a variety of religious backgrounds it may be necessary to ex-plain that the religious services are not 'real' but part of the role-play.

11.  Pupils could research and prepare a Victorian lunch e.g water or cold tea and bread and dripping or a raw carrot to eat.  These would, of course, be in authentic wrappings (e.g. a plain, white cloth) and a suitable container such as an old beer bottle or a plastic bottle disguised with papier mache or brown paper.

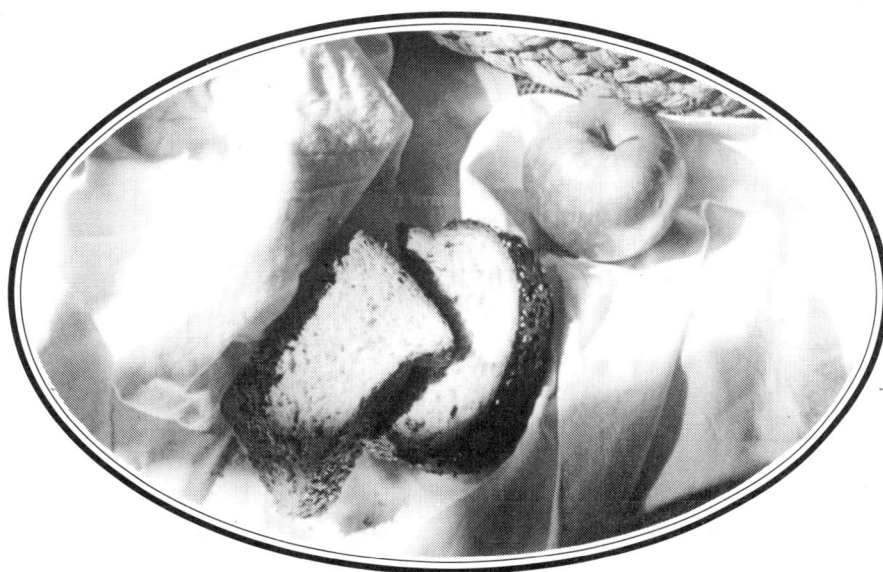

## DRESS

For evidence, look at old photographs. A good resource for ideas would be a montage of Victorian people made up of pictures from newspapers and magazines; old birthday cards showing reproduction 19th century paintings; Victorian type wrapping paper and suitable postcards. (One point to notice is that short or even rolled up sleeves are rare. If sleeves are short they seem to be either puffed sleeves, for girls, or wide sleeves reaching almost to the elbow, for boys.) Avoid obviously man-made fibres, bright colours and modern patterns.
Suitable patterns for costume are included in the (optional) accompanying Resource Folder.

Victorian clothes were often thick, heavy and uncomfortable to wear. Schools and houses were cold and draughty and it was advised that children should wear three layers of clothes. Sometimes they were sewn into their flannel underclothes for the winter. No wonder teachers complained about badly ventilated rooms.

Victorian garments were not so easy to launder as modern clothes and when washing was done without any modern aids it caused a lot of work. This explains why pinafores were worn and children reprimanded if they got dirty. There were no wellington boots then, so after the long walk to school in bad weather many pupils would have had to spend the day in wet shoes. Mufflers and fingerless gloves can look effective.

N.B. Everyone, including children, habitually wore a hat when they went out, whatever the season. It gave protection in all weather conditions and was often a sign of respectability and being properly dressed. Remember that men and boys should remove their hats on coming indoors and when greeting people outdoors.

**Male teachers** should wear, for preference:

Black tail coat or a black frock coat (bought in Oxfam or borrowed from a drama group) but any dark jacket could suffice.
Dark waistcoat.
Dark trousers.
White shirt and stiff, stand-up 'wing' collar
Neck tie or a small, silk scarf ued as a cravat.
Top hat (original, bought from a stage shop or possibly made from stiff black card) - useful for an authentic look on special occasions.
Dark socks and dark, leather shoes.
Details such as a watch chain or old spectacles would help.

N.B. A mortar board and gown is not appropriate in an elementary school since the headteacher would almost certainly not have had a university degree.


**Female teachers** need:

Long black or plain, dark coloured Victorian style dress or, failing that, a dark, plain Laura Ashley type blouse and a long, dark skirt (to give the impression of a dress).
N.B. A white blouse and dark skirt is Edwardian rather than Victorian.
Suitable dark coloured shawl or short fitted jacket.
Shoes, which need to be dark and flat, worn with dark, thick tights.
The hair fastened up or drawn off the face.
Minimal makeup, or none at all.
A lace cap or other hat (could be home-made, but check photographic evidence).
'Props' such as Victorian jewellery, spectacles or keys attached to the belt, but remember that Victorian teachers were not well paid.

**Boys** can wear:

Dark jacket or waistcoat
'Grandad' shirt (cut off the collar from a ragged, old shirt) or a long-sleeved white or grey school shirt but not a jumper, tee shirt nor a track suit top (unless it is worn under the shirt for warmth and does not show).
Dark school trousers (avoid jeans or tracksuit trousers)
Dark socks into which the trousers can be tucked.
*Alternatives:*
> sailor collar,
> jacket and stiff white 'eton' collar
> countryman's smock.

Muffler or neckerchief (worn inside the shirt collar to keep it clean)
Fingerless gloves
Baker boy cap (made in segments) can be worn, but would have been removed before entering the schoolroom. A modern man's cap is not authentic.
Dark leather shoes (if unavailable children could consider coming barefoot).
Hair could be parted and plastered down unless boys are obviously urchins.
Ragged clothes could be worn.

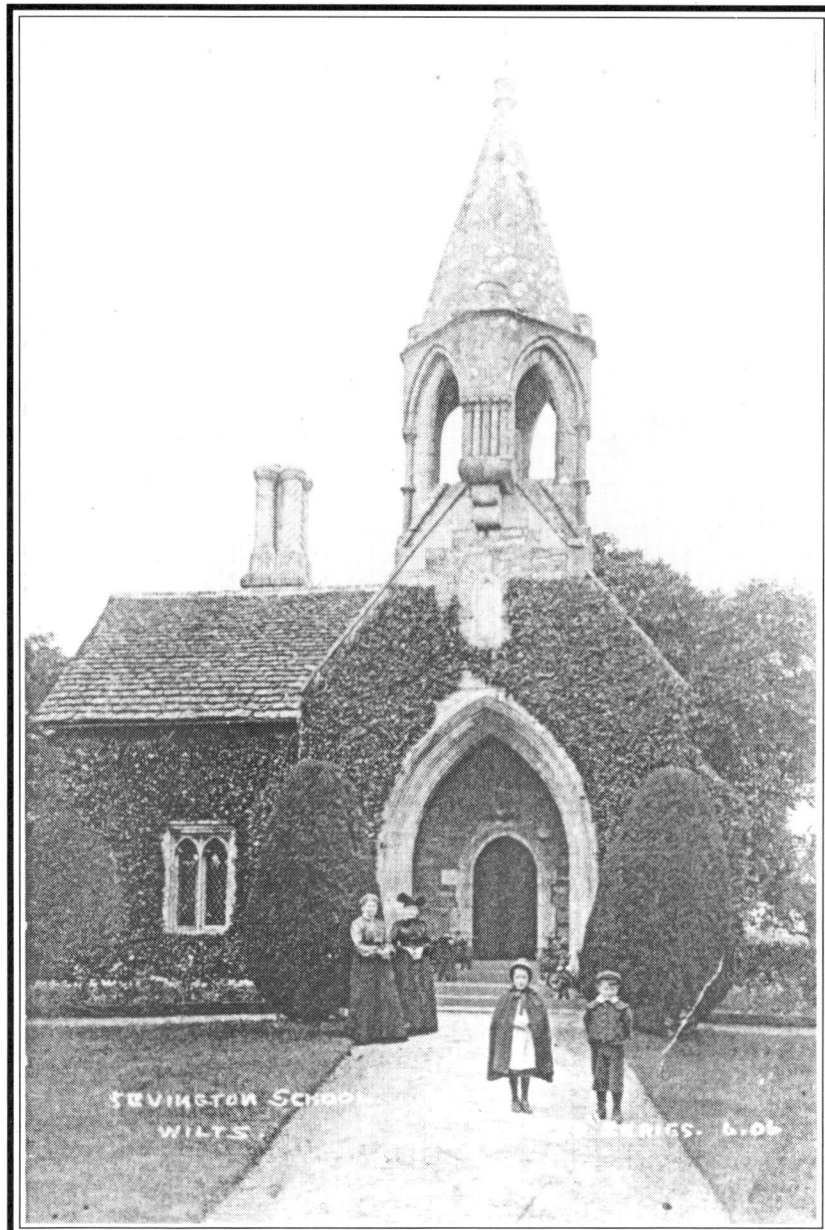

**Girls** look most authentic in:

Pinafore *worn over*
Long sleeved blouse and dark calf length skirt *or*
Longish dress which is plain and dark or which has a small flowered print.
(Remember that most children at a national school would have been very poorly dressed in shabby, torn hand-me-downs that did not fit. The wearing of bridesmaid's dresses, unless made of cotton and extremely plain, should be discouraged since such clothes would not have been worn by poorer children. Such dresses would be suitable for the daughters of the local gentry or middle classes who would have attended a private school or have been taught at home by a governess.)
Flat, dark, leather shoes or boots
Plain knee length socks or thick tights
Hair, if long, should be tied back off the face with a plain hair ribbon at the nape of the neck. A section of the hair can be gathered up and tied with a ribbon high on the back of the head but a full pony tail is not authentic. Hair can be plaited (but no French plaiting). Girls who have long hair might choose to tie it in rags the night before to have ringlets.
Cotton sunbonnet or straw hat.

**All pupils** should be asked to leave at home watches, plastic hair ornaments and other 20th-century items. Jewellery, nail varnish, sweat bands etc. are inappropriate.
Each child would have been expected to bring a cotton rag or handkerchief, possibly pinned to the clothes. Paper tissues are not acceptable.

N.B. If any pupil has a sticking-plaster visible it should be covered with a cotton bandage or rag.

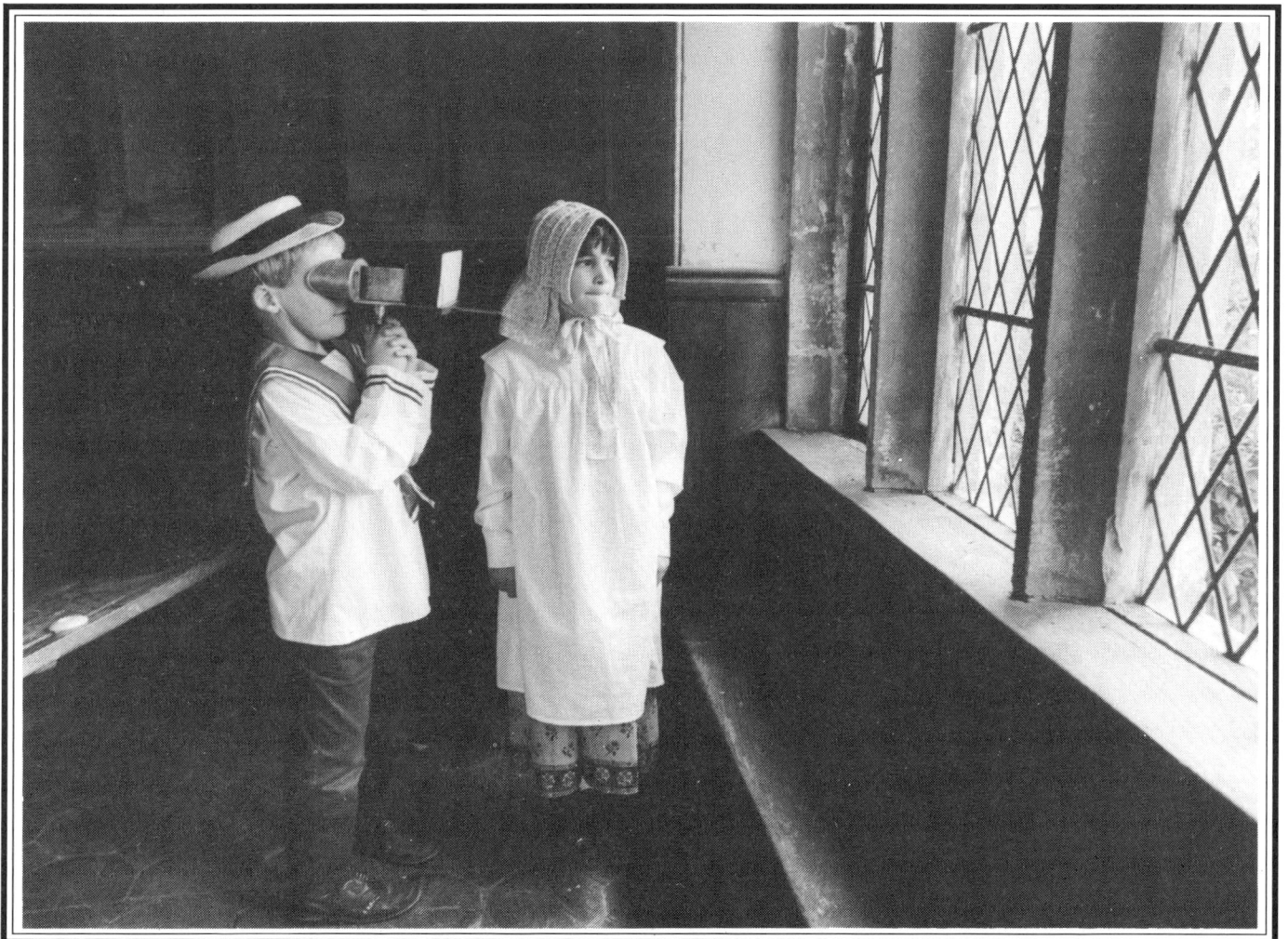

# TAKING ON ANOTHER ROLE

Many schools which are doing detailed work on the Victorians allocate real names and roles based on their own research. They often choose a particular year in which the event is to happen. A study of local trade directories, such as Kelly's, and census returns and school registers could lead to the adoption of the identities of particular children who actually lived and once attended the school at that date. Thus a child who took on the role of the blacksmith's son would need to know where he lived, his route to school, the names of other members of his family and all about his father's trade. This would give a purpose to individual research and the practice of history skills.

If several teachers are taking part in the schoolday, try to give each a specific task as well as a clearly defined role such as school inspector or, if young enough, pupil teacher. An extra parent could take on a 'visiting' role such as of vicar's daughter come to oversee the girls' needlework.

N.B. If a Victorian schoolday is being organised as part of a serious study of nineteenth century education, everybody involved should be made aware of the difference between role-play or 'history through drama' and a pageant or show. In the former an audience would not be appropriate. All those participating, including adults such as parent helpers, need to be in costume and in role. They should understand that this is a spontaneous, unrehearsed but carefully prepared event with clear objectives. The main focus is on evidence: role-play is used to link the essentially abstract nature of the children's research with the reality of everyday Victorian life and thought.

|  |  | 2nd day of October 1893 | | | | | | |
|---|---|---|---|---|---|---|---|---|
| | | A          D          M          I          S          S          I | | | | | | |
| Date of Admission | Date of Re-Admission | CHILD'S NAME IN FULL | Date of Birth | | | NAME OF PARENT OR GUARDIAN | ADDRESS | Whether exempt from Religious Instruction |
| Day Mth Year | Day Mth Year | | Day | Mth | Year | | | |
| 24 10 90 | | Welford Harry | 8 | 5 | 80 | Mr J Welford (brother) | 42 Elgar Road | No |
| 19 1 91 | | Franklin Sydney | 26 | 6 | 82 | Thomas | 81 Brunswick St | . |
| 5 10 88 | | Lockett John | 2 | 10 | 81 | Mrs Fulbrook | 6 Finch's Buildings | " |
| 14 11 89 | | Whetman Charles | 21 | 5 | 80 | Thomas | "The Grapes" Josier St | " |
| 9 11 91 | | Ashby William | 26 | 8 | 81 | William | Southcote Lane | " |
| 9 11 91 | | Vincent George | 4 | 11 | 81 | Robert | 23 Boarded Lane | " |
| 3 12 88 | | Woodley Charles | 20 | 12 | 80 | Alfred | 6 Western Road | " |
| 25 | | Lovegrove Wal. H. | | | | William | 9 Willow Street | " |
| 29 10 88 | | Stevens Edward | 31 | 3 | 81 | Richard | 24 Parnell Street | " |
| 12 1 92 | | Franklin Arthur | 10 | 9 | 81 | Kate Pavinot | 13 Lavender Street | " |
| 3 12 88 | | Brind William | 15 | 12 | 80 | George | Southcote Lane | " |
| 21 8 88 | | Rhoades James | 30 | 6 | 80 | Charles Edward | "Boars Hd" Pier St | " |
| 14 10 87 | | Davis John | 21 | 1 | 80 | James | 54 Castle Street | " |
| 12 12 92 | | Hart Fredk C.J. | 25 | 12 | 81 | William | 68 Castle Street | " |
| 10 6 93 | | Watson Roland | 21 | 5 | 81 | James | 83 Brunswick St | " |

*An extract from a school's admissions register.*

## VICTORIAN BEHAVIOUR

### The Pupils

1. Children should be seen and not heard.

2. They should not speak unless they are spoken to.

3. If asked a question they should stand up before replying.

4. Pupils should address the schoolmistress/master as 'ma'am' or 'sir' and curtsey or bow when wishing her/him good morning or good afternoon.

5. Whenever an adult enters the room they should all stand and greet him or her appropriately in unison.

6. They must do as they are told instantly.

7. When not working they should sit with their arms folded or behind their backs, according to instructions.

8. They should sit or stand up straight with shoulders back, chest out and head up.

9. They must not turn round unless ordered to do so, nor must they smile or look at other pupils.

10. All pupils should have clean hands and shoes.

11. Boys and girls line up and enter the room separately and stand behind their seats which are on opposite sides of the room. They do not sit down until instructed to do so.

12. They must march everywhere, with straight backs, and swing their arms rhythmically.

13. Even lessons were organised rigidly like drill and no-one was allowed to move or touch anything until the instruction was given. All the pupils had to obey orders instantly and at the same time e.g. Unfold your arms! Open your copybook! Pick up your pencil! Begin work now! (As well as being a way of controlling large classes this training was also partly intended to prepare children for work, where absolute obedience would be required.)

14. Pupils were not normally allowed to leave the room for any reason whilst a lesson was in progress e.g. an individual request to 'use the offices' (a euphemism for going to the earth closet) would not be looked upon with sympathy, since the whole class was expected to effect this at the appointed time.

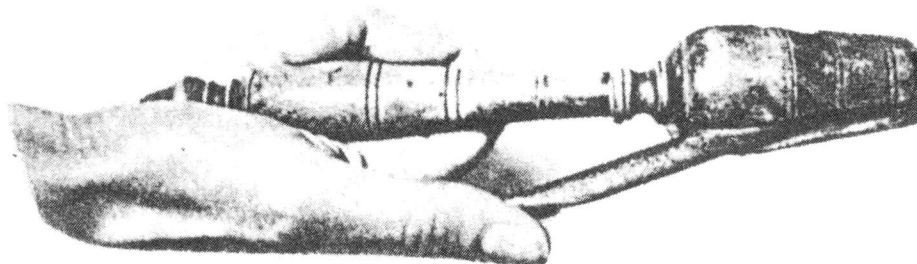

*A clicker to gain the pupils' attention.*

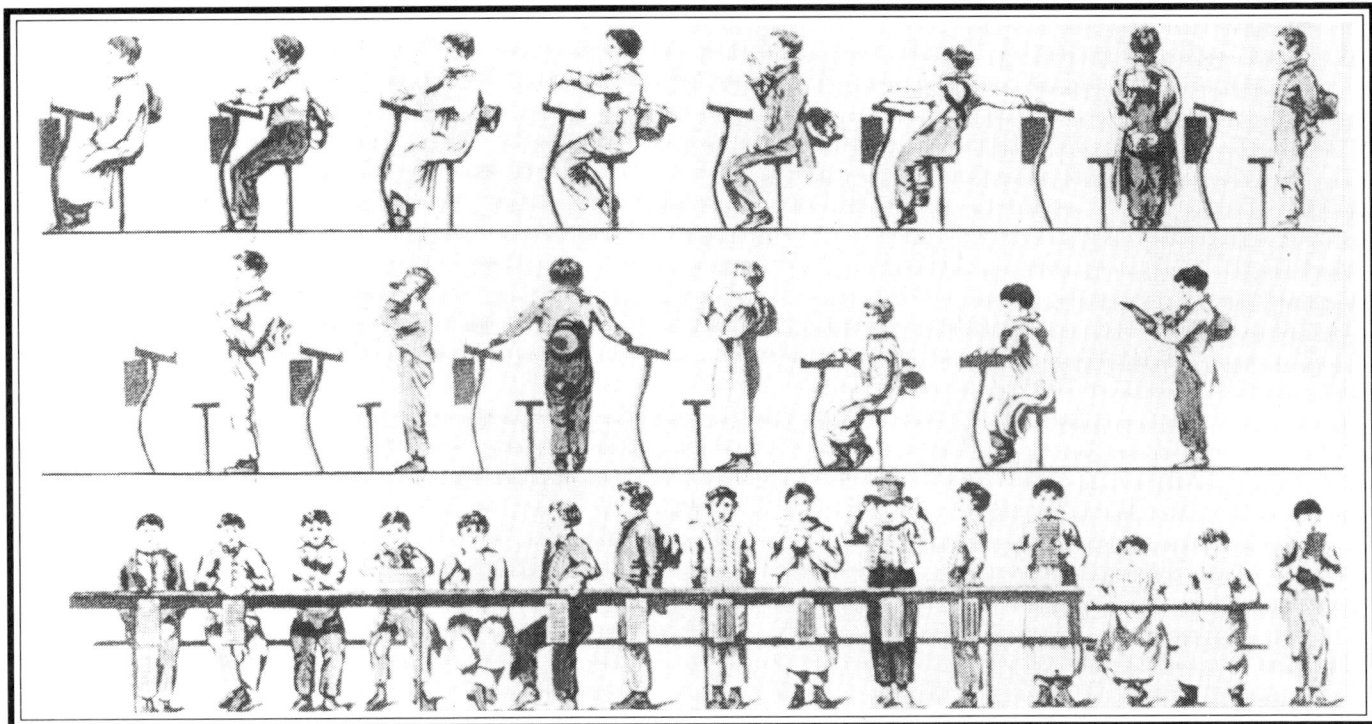

## OF BEHAVIOUR AT SCHOOL.

1. Behave to your teachers with humility, and to your school-fellows with respect.

2. Do not run into the school, but advance decently to the door.

3. When you enter, take your hat off, make your bow, or courtesy and walk straight to your seat.

4. Never talk in the school; for it interrupts yourself and others.

5. If a stranger comes in, rise, and bow or courtesy as he passes by you; then sit down, and keep your eyes upon your book, not regarding that any are present.

6. If you have any thing to say to the master, wait till he is at leisure, then speak with modesty and plainness.

7. Observe nothing at school but your book, and never neglect that.

8. Never quarrel in school; for it shows idleness and a bad temper.

9. When the master speaks to you, rise up to hear him, and look him in the face as he speaks, with modesty and attention.

10. Begin not to answer before he has done speaking; then bow to him respectfully, and answer him with humility.

11. If you have occasion to complain of a school-fellow, first speak to him softly, and desire him to desist.

12. If he will not, then rise up, and wait an opportunity; and when the master or usher's eye is upon you, bow, and say softly, and in a few words, what your complaint is.

13. Never speak loud in school. Answer a question modestly; and repeat your lesson distinctly.

14. When a stranger is in the school, do not stare at him.

15. If he speaks to the master or usher, governess or teacher, do not listen to his discourse; for that is ill manners, and shows you neglect your own business to mind others.

16. If he speaks to you, rise and hear him.

17. When he has done speaking, bow, and make a short and modest answer, and let your looks and gesture show respect.

18. When the school hours are over, go out as you came in, quietly softly, and decently.

19. Never run or crowd to get at the door; for it will be free for you after a short waiting.

**School Rules**

The list below could be read out or referred to.

# RULES FOR PUPILS.

### I.
Prepare your lessons carefully.

### II.
Come *regularly* and *punctually* to SchooL

### III.
Be as *tidy* as possible in your dress.

### IV.
If you do not understand what is taught, ask your Teacher to explain it.

### V.
Be *respectful* and *attentive* to your Teachers, and remember how kind it is of them to take so much trouble with you.

### VI.
Speak the *truth* at all costs.

### VII.
Be respectful and obedient to your Parents, Guardians, Teachers, and all set over you.

### VIII.
Study to be polite and courteous to all, avoiding coarseness and rudeness.

### IX.
Fight against *selfishness, anger,* and *all* evil.

### X.
Be kind and obliging to every one.

## The Teacher

1. The teacher's role-play should be impeccable for this sets the standard for the pupils' involvement. The value of the experience depends on total seriousness and any archness or hint of collusion about a shared joke can ruin the whole atmosphere. After all, the aim is that the children should actually experience something of what it was like to attend a Victorian school and even to feel a certain apprehension.

2. The teacher should stand very straight with head up, shoulders back and hands linked in front or behind.

3. Avoid smiling and keep a very stern face throughout.

4. Whenever appropriate use very formal language and more varied and complex words and sentences than normal. Avoid modern expressions such as 'O.K'. Here are some useful phrases which you could either use yourself or make the children chant in unison or copy from the board i.e.
   'Speech is silver, silence is golden'
   'Children should be seen and not heard'
   'The devil finds work for idle hands'
   'You cannot make a silk purse out of a sow's ear'
   'More haste, less speed'
   'Each child should understand that there is a time for work and a time for play. Every minute of time in school must be spent in work'
   'If a thing is worth doing, it is worth doing well'
   'Never put off until tomorrow what should be done today'
   'Procrastination is the thief of time'
   'Cleanliness comes next to Godliness'
   'Empty pitchers make the most noise'
   'Time and tide wait for no man'
   'A stitch in time saves nine'
   'Tut tut, Woe betide anyone who ...........'

5. Discipline was harsh in Victorian schools and beatings were commonplace. Clearly there is a limit to the lengths one can, or should, go to in the search for authenticity. The level of strictness and the amount of simulated punishment should be finely judged for each class. Obviously the pupils need to gain awareness of the daily fear with which Victorian pupils lived, but we don't want to terrify them so that they end up in tears. (The younger the children, the more likely this is). It is often a good idea to warn a pupil in advance that he or she is to be picked on for a 'punishment' and to introduce this near the end of the session so that the others are not in fear and trembling for long after this.   On the other hand, some top juniors occasionally 'get the giggles' at this point - another reason for drawing the event to a quick conclusion. Realistic punishments would be to make the pupil stand in the corner or face the wall, to wear the dunce's cap or a placard around the neck stating the misdemeanour. If a pupil is to be 'caned' this can be simulated outside the door with appropriate sound effects or by pretending to hit the pupil, who faces the class with hands on knees, but actually hitting the floor.

6. Bang on the desk or the blackboard with a pointer to get attention.

7. Pupils who begin to show signs of restlessness can be made to sit with their hands on their heads or with them folded behind their backs.

8. As part of the role-play the teacher can feed in bits of information e.g. reference could be made to the system of payment by results by warning the children to do their best when the inspector comes to test them. They could let it be known that some children were so ill-nourished that they hadn't the strength to concentrate properly and were susceptible to disease. The teacher can also let drop facts about social conditions at the time in institutions such as the workhouse.

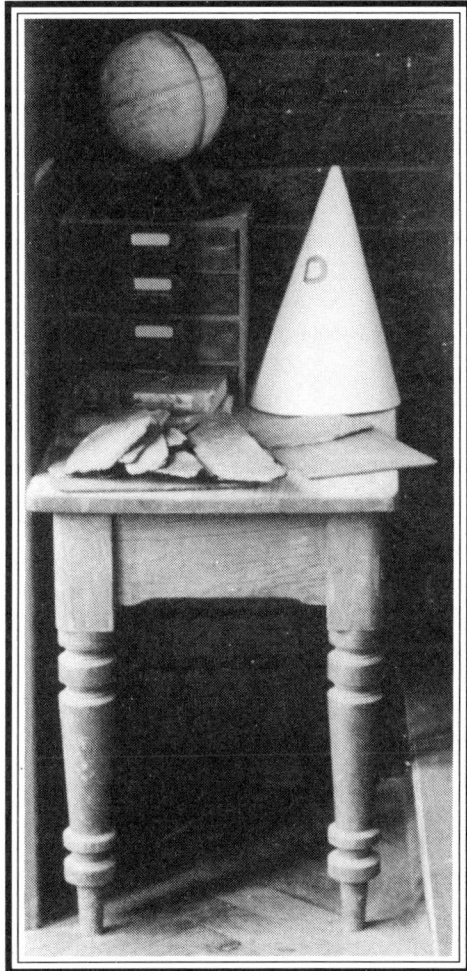

## THE TIMETABLE

The job of the elementary school was to teach the three basic subjects - reading, writing and arithmetic. These were often done early in the day before the chidren became tired. However, teachers were also encouraged, by the offer of a grant, to provide additional subjects like history or science.

If there was a wide age range, with children of several standards in one room, there could be 2 or 3 lessons going on concurrently e.g. sewing, geometric drawing and a story being read to the younger pupils.

Of course, it was easier to control a large class if everyone was doing the same thing at the same time.

The school hours varied according to local factors but 9 - 12 and 1.30 or 2 until 4 were common and children usually went home during the long dinner break. There would have been a short break in both morning and afternoon. Also drill provided an opportunity for some movement during these very static lessons.

Note that, at playtime in many schools, the boys and girls were expected to stay in separate areas in the playground. Also this is a chance to encourage traditional rhymes and games. It could be pointed out that hoops would have been bowled along the ground, not swung around the body 'in an unseemly manner'. Toys should be made of natural materials for authenticity.

*Here is a possible timetable, but you could make up one of your own:*

Register, collection of pennies and hand/shoe inspection.
Prayer, hymn, bible reading and moral homily.
Tables chanted.
Sums from the board, on slates.
Reading lesson.
Spellings chanted.
> *Break.*

Writing in copybooks with dip-in pen and ink.
Drill.
Geography.
> *Dinner Break.*

Religious instruction or Bible story.
History.
Sewing for girls and Geometric Drawing for boys.
> *Break.*

Poetry and Recitation.
Object lesson.
Presentation of certificates.
Prayer.

## IV. Distribution of Time.

**1. In Infant Department.**—This will depend upon the class. Supposing the school hours to be twenty-five, we get something like the following :—

1. Registration, religious observances, religious instruction, 4 ⅛ hours.
2. Recreation, 2½ hours.
3. Arithmetic, 3½ hours.
4. Reading, 3½ hours.
5. Writing, 3 hours.
6. Needlework, 2 hours 50 minutes.
7. Object Lessons, 1 hour 40 minutes.
8. Singing, 1 hour.
9. Spelling, ½ hour.
*10. Kindergarten, 1 hour.
11. Drill, 50 minutes.
12. Recitation, 30 minutes.

This distribution of time would be approximate only in the babies' class, as these little ones would have a Kindergarten lesson each day, as well as an extra lesson in Singing and Recitation on Needlework days. The Arithmetic would be taken directly after Religious Instruction, as the children are then most capable of mental effort. The object lesson would therefore be given each morning for the same reason. Singing, Needlework, Recitation, and Kindergarten are the most suitable for the afternoon. The fifty minutes for drill allows five minutes sharp exercise each morning. This exercise immediately preceding the object lesson, and for a lesson of twenty-five minutes' duration once a week.

*N.B. Kindergarten, recently introduced from Germany, meant learning through toys and play.*

Here is a timetable, based on a modern school's own records and intended for its centenary celebrations.

Why not make up one suited to your own circumstances and needs?

## Wanborough Board School - 1881

**A.M.**

9.15 - 9.30. ~ Registration, Examination of hands and shoes. Prayers with Lesson.

9.30 ~ 10.00 ~ Tables by rote, followed by formal Scripture

10.00 ~ 10.30 ~ Formal Arithmetic from black board. Attention to layout, figure formation and correction of errors.

10.30 ~ 10.45 ~ ~ ~ ~ Playtime

10.45 ~ 11.15 ~ Music Practice
Shepherd songs etc. The Imperial Songs shown in the School Log Book for 1887

11.15 ~ 12.00 ~ Cursive Writing Practice and Formal Grammar
Lunchtime

**P.M.**

1.15 ~ 2.30 ~ Art ~ perspective drawing. Copying a flower or leaf; looking for detail, not design.
Drill ~ formal exercises on the playground.
{ If wet Geography or History }

2.30 ~ 2.40 ~ ~ ~ ~ Playtime

2.40 ~ ~ ~ Nature Study
Poetry
Story - extract from "The Water Babies"

3.30 ~ ~ Close school with Prayers.

## ORGANISING THE DAY

Boys and girls line up separately outside the room or in the playground. This should be according to size, age, alphabetical order or which standard they are in. They stand upright, without speaking, and march into the classroom at a command. They stand behind their seats until they have been greeted by the teacher. After they have replied with 'Good morning, ma'am/sir' they are told to sit down with 'Class be seated'.

### THE REGISTER

It is more authentic if pupils have Victorian names. These could be researched in an old school register or chosen from those in Appendix III. Boys and girls were listed separately and when each child's full name is called he/she stands and says 'Present, ma'am' (or 'sir').

When calling the register take the opportunity to let the pupils know reasons for absence e.g. serious illness such as diphtheria, possibly resulting in death; truancy due to pressure from the parents to earn extra money or staying at home to help the mother following her fifteenth confinement. Impassable roads due to bad weather, might have prevented a pupil's walking the usual three miles to school. (At this point you might consult your own records to introduce reasons which provide local colour.) Children who do not attend regularly can be threatened with the board man who was sent by the School Board to the child's home to find out the reason for absence. Pupils were punished for both unpunctuality and absenteeism, even when not their own fault.

You could record the numbers present and absent on the attendance board and extol the virtues of being 'Never absent, never late'.

(It is worth noting that some children started school as young as 2 years old if their mothers had a large family or needed to go out to work.)

*Extract from the sick list of William Street School, Swindon:*

| Batt Herbert | II | Infdammation of eyes with debility . . . . . |
| Page Richard | IV | Rheumatism with slow fever . . . . |
| Kempton Walter | IV | Low Fever . . . . . . Died 19. Sept. . |
| Ball Herbert | II | Rheumatism with fever . . . . . . |

### THE COLLECTION OF SCHOOL PENNIES

Voluntary schools found they had to charge children a few pennies per week to help defray costs. (The amount varied from school to school.)

Children who attended 'Board Schools', set up by the local school board after 1870, were expected to pay school fees of 2 pence a week, although poor families were often excused. The charge was made to supplement the often inadequate support which came from the local councils via the rates. You may wish to include the collection of school fees in your Victorian schoolday. If so Victorian pennies can be acquired fairly readily at junk/antique shops and could be worth buying if a Victorian schoolday is to be a regular occurrence. However, such school fees were abolished in 1891.

### INSPECTION

The teacher might like to make an inspection of hands, nails or shoes.

**PRAYERS**

Here are a few suitable opening prayers including the older version of the Lord's Prayer. Children can repeat each line after the teacher. If there are pupils in the class from different religious backgrounds, the word 'Lord' could apply to whichever deity the children usually address and the phrase 'Jesus Christ' could be missed out.

### A MORNING PRAYER

*Grant us, O Lord to pass this day in gladness and peace, without stumbling and without stain, that, reaching the eventide victorious over all temptations. we may praise thee, the eternal God, who art blessed and dost govern all things, Word without end, Amen.*

*(Mozarabic - Ancient Spanish)*

*O Lord. our Heavenly Father, Almighty and everlasting God, who hast safely brought us to the beginning of another day; defend us in the same with Thy mighty power; and grant that this day we fall into no sin, neither into any kind of danger; but that all our doings may be ordered by Thy governance, to do always that which is righteous in Thy sight; through Jesus Christ, our Lord. Amen.*

### SCHOOL PRAYER

*Bless, O Lord, we beseech thee,*
*This our school.*
*Take away whatsoever is unworthy,*
*Cherish and strengthen whatsoever is best in it;*
*And grant that all who go forth hence*
*May manfully fight Thy battles in the world*
*And conquer, through thy might.*          *Amen.*

### THE PRAYER OF IGNATIUS LOYOLA

*Teach us, Good Lord, to serve Thee as Thou deservest;*
*to give, and not to count the cost;*
*to fight and not to heed the wounds;*
*to toil and not to seek for rest;*
*to labour and not to ask for any reward,*
*save that of knowing that we do Thy will.*          *Amen.*

*O eternal God who watchest over us all, grant that the friendships*
*formed between us here may neither through sin be broken, nor*
*here-after through worldly cares be forgotten, but that,*
*bound together by the unseen chain of love,*
*we may draw nearer to Thee and nearer to each other;*
*through Jesus Christ, Our Lord.*          *Amen.*

*Our Father, which art in heaven, Hallowed be Thy name.*
*Thy kingdom come, Thy will be done, on earth, as it is in heaven.*
*Give us this day our daily bread. And forgive us our trespasses,*
*as we forgive them that trespass against us.*
*And lead us not into temptation but deliver us from evil:*
*For Thine is the kingdom, the power and the glory.*
*For ever and ever.*          *Amen.*

**HYMNS**

Hymns of a suitable date could include *'All things bright and beautiful'* and *'Jesus, friend of little children'*.

ALL THINGS BRIGHT AND BEAUTIFUL (KEATS) (*First Tune*).
*Verse* 1 *and* REFRAIN. 7.6.7.6. and refrain. W. H. MONK, 1823-89.

3 The purple-headed mountain,
   The river running by,
The sunset and the morning,
   That brightens up the sky :

4 The cold wind in the winter,
   The pleasant summer sun,
The ripe fruits in the garden,—
   He made them every one :

5 The tall trees in the greenwood,
   The meadows for our play,
The rushes by the water,
   To gather every day :

6 The rich man in his castle,
   The poor man at his gate,
God made them high or lowly,
   And ordered their estate.

7 He gave us eyes to see them,
   And lips that we might tell
How great is God Almighty,
   Who has made all things well!

27

## GENTLE JESUS, MEEK AND MILD

1 GENTLE Jesus, meek and mild,
Look upon a little child,
Pity my simplicity,
Suffer me to come to Thee.

2 Fain I would to Thee be brought ;
Gracious Lord, forbid it not ;
In the kingdom of Thy grace
Give a little child a place.

3 Fain I would be as Thou art ;
Give me Thy obedient heart :
Thou art pitiful and kind ;
Let me have Thy loving mind.

4 Let me above all fulfil
God my heavenly Father's will ;
Never His good Spirit grieve,
Only to His glory live.

5 Lamb of God, I look to Thee ;
Thou shalt my example be :
Thou art gentle, meek, and mild ;
Thou wast once a little child.

6 Thou didst live to God alone ;
Thou didst never seek Thine own ;
Thou Thyself didst never please :
God was all Thy happiness.

7 Loving Jesus, gentle Lamb,
In Thy gracious hands I am :
Make me, Saviour, what Thou art ;
Live Thyself within my heart.

8 I shall then show forth Thy praise,
Serve Thee all my happy days ;
Then the world shall always see
Christ, the holy Child, in me.

*Charles Wesley,* 1707-88.

*     *     *     *

## BIBLE READING

The King James Bible would have been used. You could read the collect for the day as listed in the Prayer Book. Alternatively, Genesis Chapter 7, vv 1-10, the 23rd Psalm or Corinthians I Chapter 13 are suitable.


## MORAL HOMILY

The teacher could expound on 'Cleanliness comes next to Godliness', making reference to the earlier hand inspection, and urging the pupils to have a clean mind as well as a clean body.

The virtue of humility might be explained. Pupils could be exhorted to accept the lowly place in society into which it has pleased God to place them and not to emulate their elders or betters. Again this was part of the training for which schools were intended i.e. to try and foster political stability through acceptance of the existing social order.

A useful rhyme for rote learning, which encourages humility is:
> *'God bless the squire and his relations*
> *And keep us in our proper stations'.*

Alternatively, you might like to draw attention to this verse from *'All things bright and beautiful'*:
> *'The rich man in his castle*
> *The poor man at his gate*
> *He made them high or lowly*
> *He ordered their estate'.*

A special word might be said to the girls, whose purpose in life was to run a home and be a dutiful and odedient wife. Phrases such as 'A woman's place is in the home' and 'Be good sweet maid, and let who can be clever' could be chanted or copied from the board. This might be an opportunuty to explain how domestic service and marriage were the two most likely options for the girls. Thus the ability to sew a neat seam is paramount.

Exhortation to work hard could be re-inforced by repeating together the following:
> *'Good, better, best*
> *Never let it rest,*
> *'Til your good is better*
> *And your better, best'.*

There could be an explanation of what is meant by the '3 Rs' and why learning to be proficient in all three could help when seeking employment e.g. a boy with a 'neat hand' might gain work as a clerk in an office.

Here one headmaster explains how he tried to inculcate various virtues in his pupils:

> Consideration for others, &c:- This is repeatedly enforced by religious instruction & exemplified in our daily treatment of the boys themselves: notice is always taken when the contrary occurs.
> Honour & Truthfulness, &c :- Among the elder boys it is impressed that every man can be a gentleman, in the higher sense of the term; that such an one will not do a dishonourable action, nor take any mean advantage; above all, will not be a liar.

**THE LESSONS**

The teacher could start by writing the date on the blackboard e.g. Monday, March 19th, 1894. The pupils could then copy it onto their slates. This is a good way of setting the schoolday firmly at some specific point in time. It is worth giving careful thought to this date e.g. you might choose a day exactly 100 years ago. But, whatever date you choose must be reflected in the role play e.g. you would not know before 1897 whether or not Queen Victoria lived to celebrate her Diamond Jubilee. You may need to refer to your time line to check dates.

Also, why not learn to recite this rhyme?

> 'Thirty days hath September,
> April, June and November
> All the rest have thirty one
> Excepting February alone
> Which has twenty eight days clear
> And twenty nine each leap year'.

Most of the lesson time was spent on reading, writing, arithmetic and religious instruction. Other subjects were done infrequently until well into the twentieth century. Although authentic, modern children would find this tedious so it is suggested that they are a given a taste of a selection of all lessons that might have been encompassed during a child's school life.

**Reading**

Children began by learning their letters, sometimes from a box of wooden blocks or from alphabet charts*. Then they progressed from easy to more difficult passsages. The first books, or primers as they were called, only contained words of one syllable as these were supposed to be less difficult. Actually many of the sentences were almost nonsense e.g. 'Lo it is so as ye go to it'. Opposite are a few pages from a 'Child's First Book' found at Sevington School. (Reproduction copies are available - see Appendix VIII.) A reading lesson can only be authentic if a facsimile reading book or (for infants) a reading chart* is available. It is better not to include this lesson if you do not have the correct equipment (single photocopied sheets of a page from a reader would not be an authentic resource). There was usually one book for each standard and when it was finished the child re-read it repeatedly. Most of the stories were improving tales and had a moral to them. They tried to impart knowledge, religion and right conduct as well as teaching reading.

*    *An alphabet chart and an infants reading chart are contained in the (optional) Resource Folder accompanying this manual.*

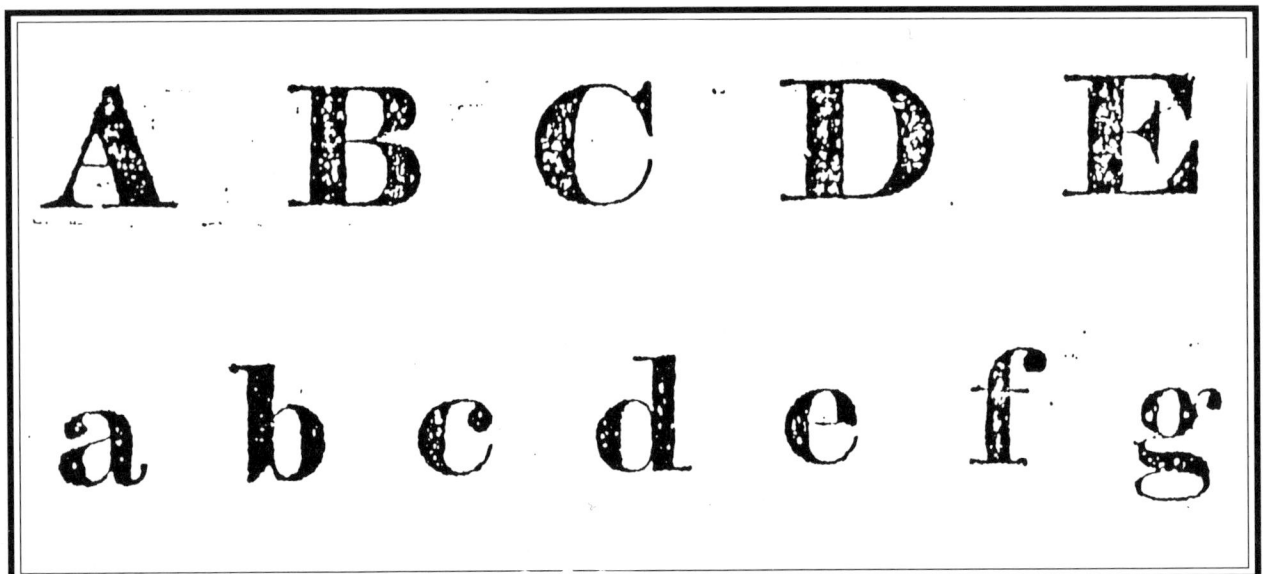

### Lesson VI.

| | |
|---|---|
| As we do | It is to be so |
| He is up | Is he to go in |
| If we do it | He is to be up |
| I am to go | Do go by it |
| Do ye so | He is by me |
| We go by it | Is he to be up |
| As if ye be | So is he to go |
| I am to do it | It is an ox |
| As I am in | If ye do go in |

### Lesson VII.

| | |
|---|---|
| So do ye | Do it to me |
| So am I | I am to go up |
| I do so by it | So it is to be |
| He is to be | Do ye be so |
| Lo I am he | I am by it |
| As we go to it | He is to go on |
| Ah me it is so | We go to an ox |
| O go ye in | It is my ox |
| Do so to us | So do ye go |

---

**Much Approved.**     **7th Edition**

# THE NEW
# READING EASY:
### Or,
## CHILD'S
# FIRST BOOK;
Arranged so as to blend
### Entertainment with Instruction.

BRADFORD, WILTS.
Printed by J. Rawlins, and sold by the Booksellers.
*Price Three-pence.*

---

#### Easy Lessons.—VI.

COME to school clean and neat ; play not by the way, nor let your voice be heard in the street.

When you are at school take your place ; make no noise, but strive to learn.

When you come to say your task, speak out plain, and mind to sound all your words right.

Be sure to mind your stops ; read from stop to stop, as you see them in the book ; and do not make a stop where there is none.

Spell such words as you can not read, and then you will know them the next time you see them.

---

#### Easy Lessons.—VII.

WHEN school is done, go strait home, and go not to play, till your friends give you leave.

Play not much at once, but come home soon, like a good child.

Be not proud of what you have, for fools may wear fine clothes, but a wise child is known by his words.

When a child who is told of a fault, says he does not care, there is much fear that he will not mend.

#### SAMMY GOOD.

I am go-ing to tell you my child the his-tory of Sam-my Good. In the first place I have to say that he was kind to his sis-ters. When lit-tle boys are kind to their sis-ters, I have al-ways found that the lit-tle girls tri-ed to make their bro-thers hap-py. He that lo-veth God, lo-veth his bro-ther also.' In this pic-ture

you see him dig-ging in his gar-den, and lit-tle Grace is rea-ding to him. I think it must be some good book, they are so atten-tive to it, per-haps it is the "New Tes-ta-ment." Do you wish to love the Sa-viour like lit-tle Grace.

This good boy had been taught that what-ever he did, he should try and do it well. "What-so-ever thy hand fin-deth to

## Writing, Dictation and Spelling

First of all the infants learned to form their letters in a sand tray, using their finger or a stick. Next they moved on to the slate on which they wrote with a slate pencil not chalk. This is a chance to use the phrase, 'Let us begin with a clean slate'. Regard for authenticity would mean that this is effected with a piece of flannel or real sponge which has been moistened with clean water. The time-honoured method of 'spit and cuff' should not be encouraged for reasons of hygiene.

*Sandtray*

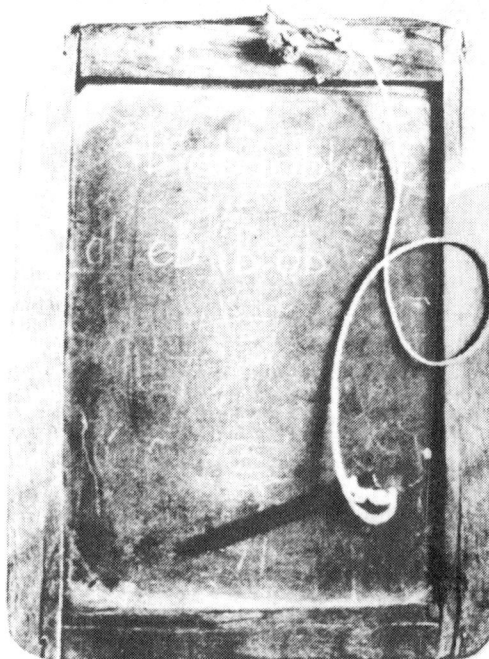

*Slate*

Finally, in the upper standards (the equivalent of today's juniors) they were sometimes given brown paper and crayons, but more usually moved straight on to dip-in pens, ink and copy-books. (It is suggested that teachers make a small copybook for each pupil, or an exercise book with a range of different types of work, since single sheets of paper would not have been used. See Appendix V for examples from a copybook.)

Some children tend to make rather a mess with dip in pens and ink, so have pen wipers and blotting paper available and maybe use washable ink. This would be a good point at which to introduce the phrase 'to blot your copybook'.

N.B. The use of paper and pencils was generally reserved for drawing since lead pencils were expensive. Pupils practised their handwriting for many hours each week. They wrote in a copybook; first going over a faint outline, then forming the letters unaided in the lines below. Once again the phrases they had to copy also encouraged the acquisition of knowledge as well as good behaviour and moral thinking.

Before the introduction of the typewriter, good handwriting was regarded as very important. The letters had to be neat, regular and well-formed. There were strict instructions about how to sit, how to hold the pen and where to position the copybook. (The pupil had to sit straight and upright at the desk. The elbow of the writing arm had to be kept close in to the body and the book had to be positioned centrally and straight on the writing surface.) Also everyone was expected to use the right hand even if naturally left-handed. Apart from an unthinking desire for conformity, the main reasons for this were practical i.e. the left hand would smudge the wet ink and also if the light came from windows on the left, as suggested in contemporary teaching manuals, using the left hand would cast a shadow onto the page.

Writing also included dictation. At first single words and then simple sentences were read out. By Standard V the teacher read out a passage which the pupils had to re-write in their own words. Only the most able pupils were allowed to write compositions using their own thoughts.

Spelling was equally mechanical and they learned words by chanting together: 'a-n-g-e-l spells angel'. Here are some contemporary spelling lists:

| An-gel | chap-man | En-ter | gos-pel | | *Dress.* | | |
|--------|----------|--------|---------|---|---|---|---|
| ab-bot | cru-el | e-vil | grit-ty | Boots | fan | mits | sash |
| ab-bey | cra-zy | e-ver | gun-ner | band | frock | muff | stock |
| ar-bour | cor-ner | em-blem | gut-ter | cloth | gloves | pins | shirt |
| ad-vent | cop-per | em-bers | gen-try | coat | gown | ring | sleeves |
| al-lum | com-fort | el-bow | gra-vy | curl | hose | stuff | silk |
| am-ber | cum-ber | Far-mer | gras-sy | cloak | hat | scarf | sock |
| ac-tor | con-cord | fe-male | Ham-mer | cap | lawn | shoes | veil |
| art-ful | com-mon | fen-der | ham-let | dress | lace | string | wigs |
| art-less | cut-ler | fod-der | han-dy | | | | |

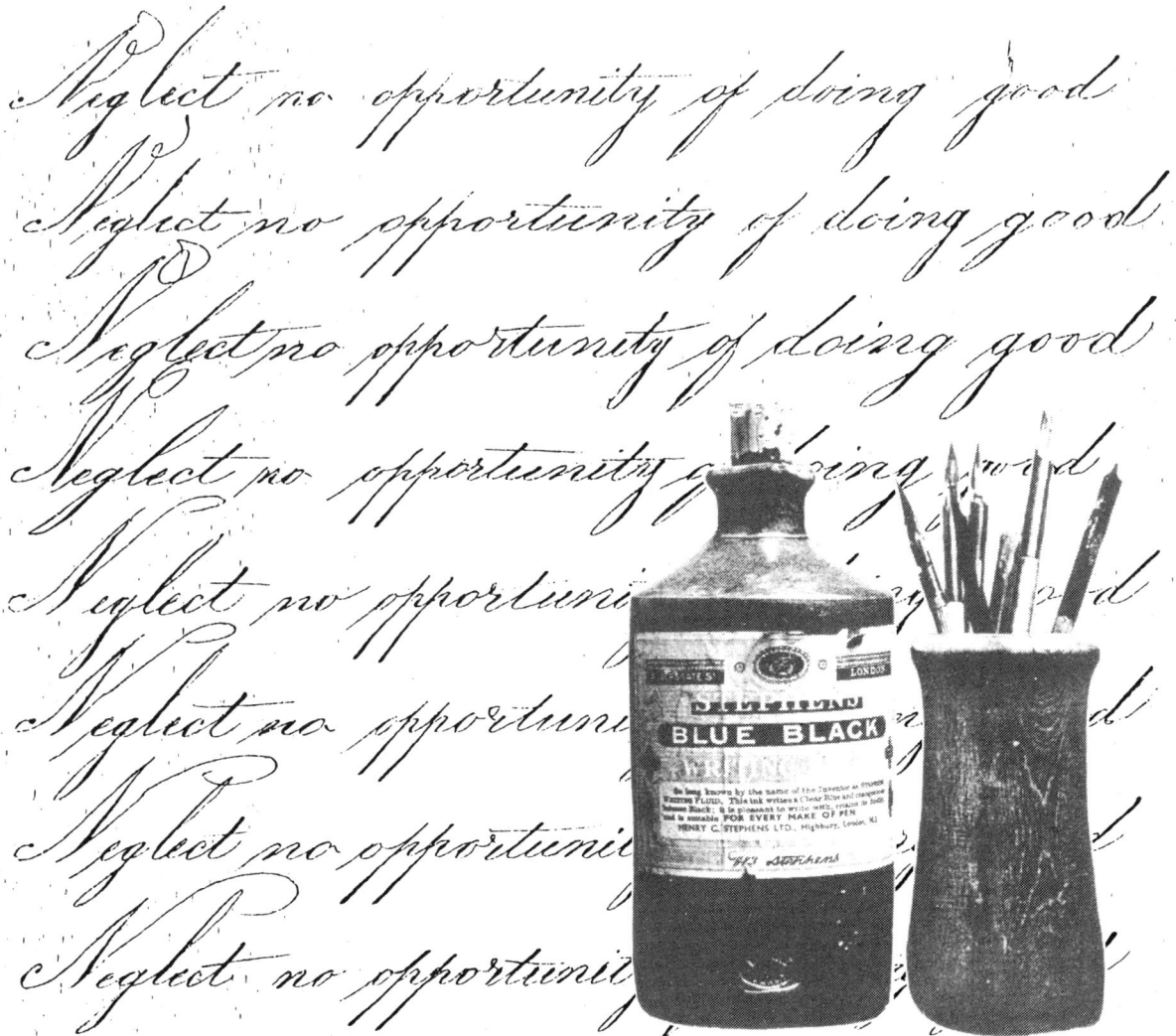

*Copybook, pens and ink bottle.*

# MULTIPLICATION TABLE.

| 2 times | 3 times | 4 times | 5 times | 6 times | 7 times | 8 times | 9 times | 10 times | 11 times | 12 times |
|---|---|---|---|---|---|---|---|---|---|---|
| 1 are 2 | 1 are 3 | 1 are 4 | 1 are 5 | 1 are 6 | 1 are 7 | 1 are 8 | 1 are 9 | 1 are 10 | 1 are 11 | 1 are 12 |
| 2... 4 | 2... 6 | 2... 8 | 2...10 | 2...12 | 2...14 | 2...16 | 2... 18 | 2... 20 | 2... 22 | 2... 24 |
| 3... 6 | 3... 9 | 3...12 | 3...15 | 3...18 | 3...21 | 3...24 | 3... 27 | 3... 30 | 3... 33 | 3... 36 |
| 4... 8 | 4...12 | 4...16 | 4...20 | 4...24 | 4...28 | 4...32 | 4... 36 | 4... 40 | 4... 44 | 4... 48 |
| 5...10 | 5...15 | 5...20 | 5...25 | 5...30 | 5...35 | 5...40 | 5... 45 | 5... 50 | 5... 55 | 5... 60 |
| 6...12 | 6...18 | 6...24 | 6...30 | 6...36 | 6...42 | 6...48 | 6... 54 | 6... 60 | 6... 66 | 6... 72 |
| 7...14 | 7...21 | 7...28 | 7...35 | 7...42 | 7...49 | 7...56 | 7... 63 | 7... 70 | 7... 77 | 7... 84 |
| 8...16 | 8...24 | 8...32 | 8...40 | 8...48 | 8...56 | 8...64 | 8... 72 | 8... 80 | 8... 88 | 8... 96 |
| 9...18 | 9...27 | 9...36 | 9...45 | 9...54 | 9...63 | 9...72 | 9... 81 | 9... 90 | 9... 99 | 9...108 |
| 10...20 | 10...30 | 10...40 | 10...50 | 10...60 | 10...70 | 10...80 | 10... 90 | 10...100 | 10...110 | 10...120 |
| 11...22 | 11...33 | 11...44 | 11...55 | 11...66 | 11...77 | 11...88 | 11... 99 | 11...110 | 11...121 | 11...132 |
| 12...24 | 12...36 | 12...48 | 12...60 | 12...72 | 12...84 | 12...96 | 12...108 | 12...120 | 12...132 | 12...144 |

**Tables**

'Twice-one-are-two, twice-two-are-four...............' Notice that tables go up to times 12 not times 10 as today.

**Arithmetic**

Sums can be copied from the blackboard. This is best done on slates so that mistakes can easily be rubbed out. In any case, make them rather easier than children are used to. If doing pound, shilling and pence sums it is simpler where there is no 'carrying' or 'borrowing' although some older, more able pupils may enjoy the challenge of this. Also this gives everyone a chance to use a slate, although in Victorian times children generally progressed to using pen and ink as they got older and moved to a higher standard.

*Standard I* - Learn numbers up to 1,000. Do easy addition, subtraction and multiplication sums. Beginners were encouraged to use the abacus to work out the answers. Counting on the fingers was discouraged but sometimes tiny sticks were used instead. Standard I children were also expected to know tables up to the six times including times eleven and twelve.
*Standard II* - Division sums
*Standard III* - Money sums
By *Standard VI* - Fractions, decimals, simple proportion and simple interest.

Here are some examples of suitable mathematical problems:

191. The population of London in 1871 was 3,251,804, and that of Nottingham was 86608. How much greater was the population of London than that of Nottingham, and how many times as great was it?

192. A ship of war captured a prize valued at £34725 ; the officers received one-third of this, and the remainder was equally divided among the crew of 486 men. What was each man's share?

193. A dealer went to market with £100, and bought as many sheep as he could at £1 12s. 8d. each. How many did he buy, and what money had he left?

Religion was even brought into arithmetic as you can see from this last question:
*If Abraham had 750 sheep and Lot had 533 sheep, how many did they have together?*

Original sums

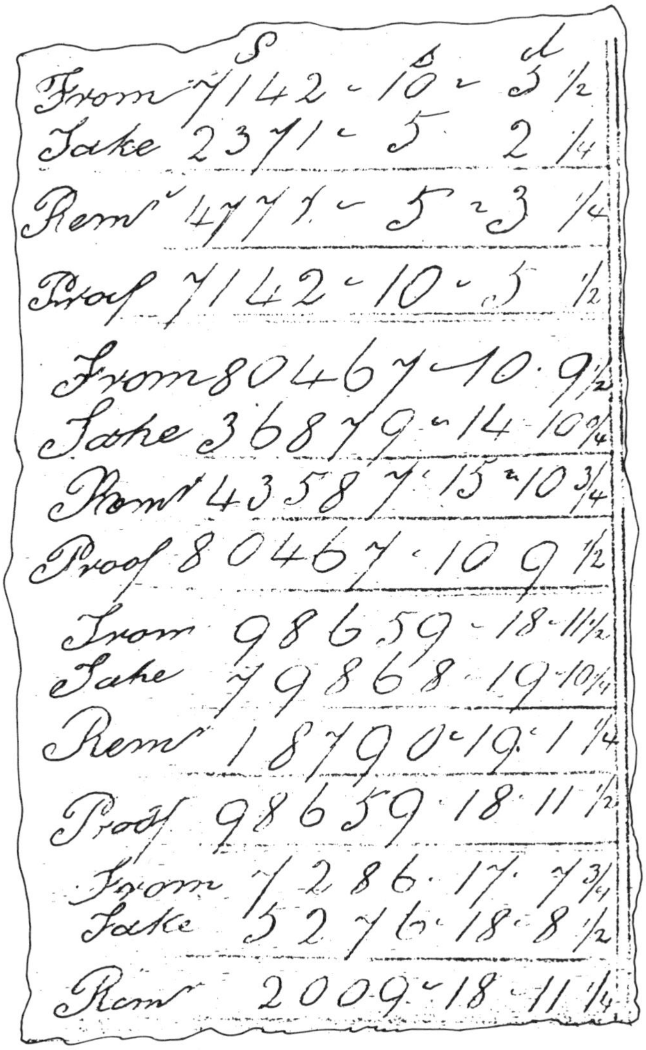

| | £ | s | d | |
|---|---|---|---|---|
| From | 7142 | 10 | 3 | ½ |
| Take | 2371 | 5 | 2 | ¼ |
| Rem | 4771 | 5 | 3 | ¼ |
| Proof | 7142 | 10 | 5 | ½ |
| From | 80467 | 10 | 9 | ½ |
| Take | 36879 | 14 | 10 | ¾ |
| Rem | 43587 | 15 | 10 | ¾ |
| Proof | 80467 | 10 | 9 | ½ |
| From | 98659 | 18 | 11 | ½ |
| Take | 79868 | 19 | 10 | ¼ |
| Rem | 18790 | 19 | 1 | ¼ |
| Proof | 98659 | 18 | 11 | ½ |
| From | 7286 | 17 | 7 | ¾ |
| Take | 5276 | 18 | 8 | ½ |
| Rem | 2009 | 18 | 11 | ¼ |

```
6 7 2 8 9   4 2 5
5 4 7 6 2   6 7 8
7 9 5 4 2   7 6 4
8 2 5 3 4   3 6 2
2 3 6 5 6   4 7 3
6 2 8 9 7   6 3 9
5 3 7 8 9   7 6 5
4 2 4 4 7 3 1 0 4
```

| £ | s | D | |
|---|---|---|---|
| 564 | 9 | 11 | ¼ |
| | | | 5 |
| 1693 | 9 | 9 | 3¼ |

Examples of work by a late 20th century child.

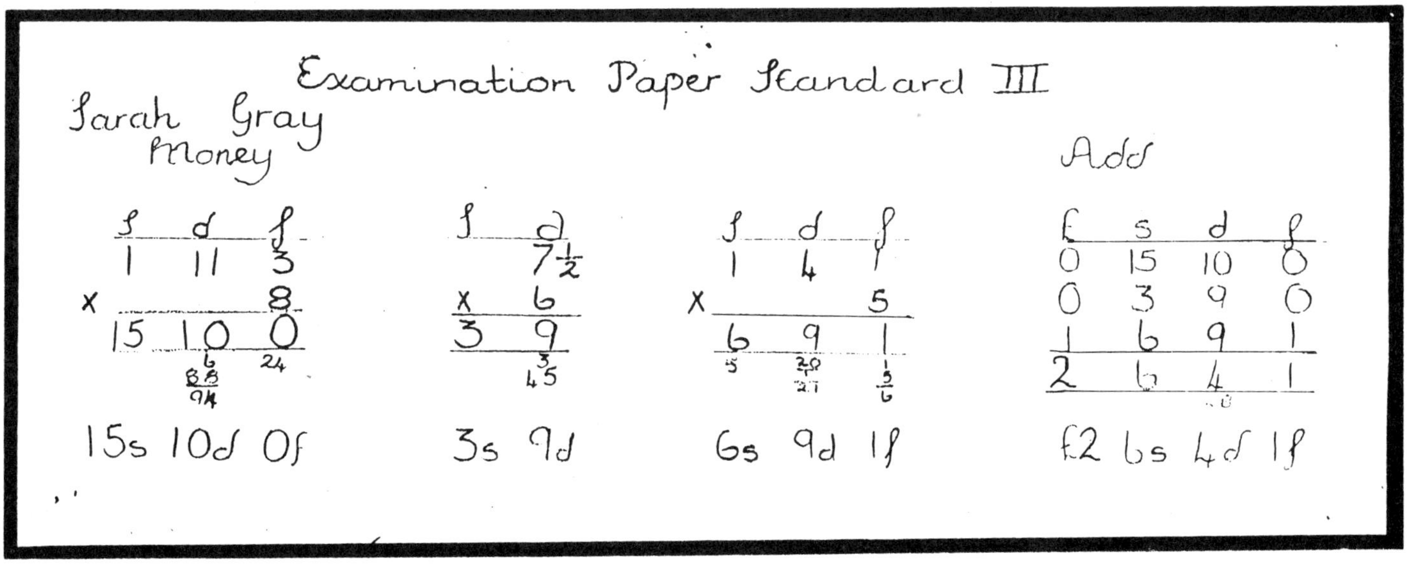

Examination Paper Standard III

Sarah Gray
Money                                                    Add

| s | d | f |
|---|---|---|
| 1 | 11 | 3 |
| × | | 8 |
| 15 | 10 | 0 |

15s 10d 0f

| s | d | f |
|---|---|---|
| | 7½ | |
| × | 6 | |
| 3 | 9 | |

3s 9d

| s | d | f |
|---|---|---|
| 1 | 4 | |
| × | | 5 |
| 6 | 9 | 1 |

6s 9d 1f

| £ | s | d | f |
|---|---|---|---|
| 0 | 15 | 10 | 0 |
| 0 | 3 | 9 | 0 |
| 1 | 6 | 9 | 1 |
| 2 | 6 | 4 | 1 |

£2 6s 4d 1f

35

## Religious Instruction

This was the most important subject, particularly in the 'National Schools' which were maintained by the Church of England. In these schools children had to learn the catechism, part of which is included here. Religious teaching in 'British' and 'Board Schools' was non-denominational. As already mentioned, special sensitivity may be needed if teaching about Victorian religious beliefs to a multi-racial, multi-denominational class.

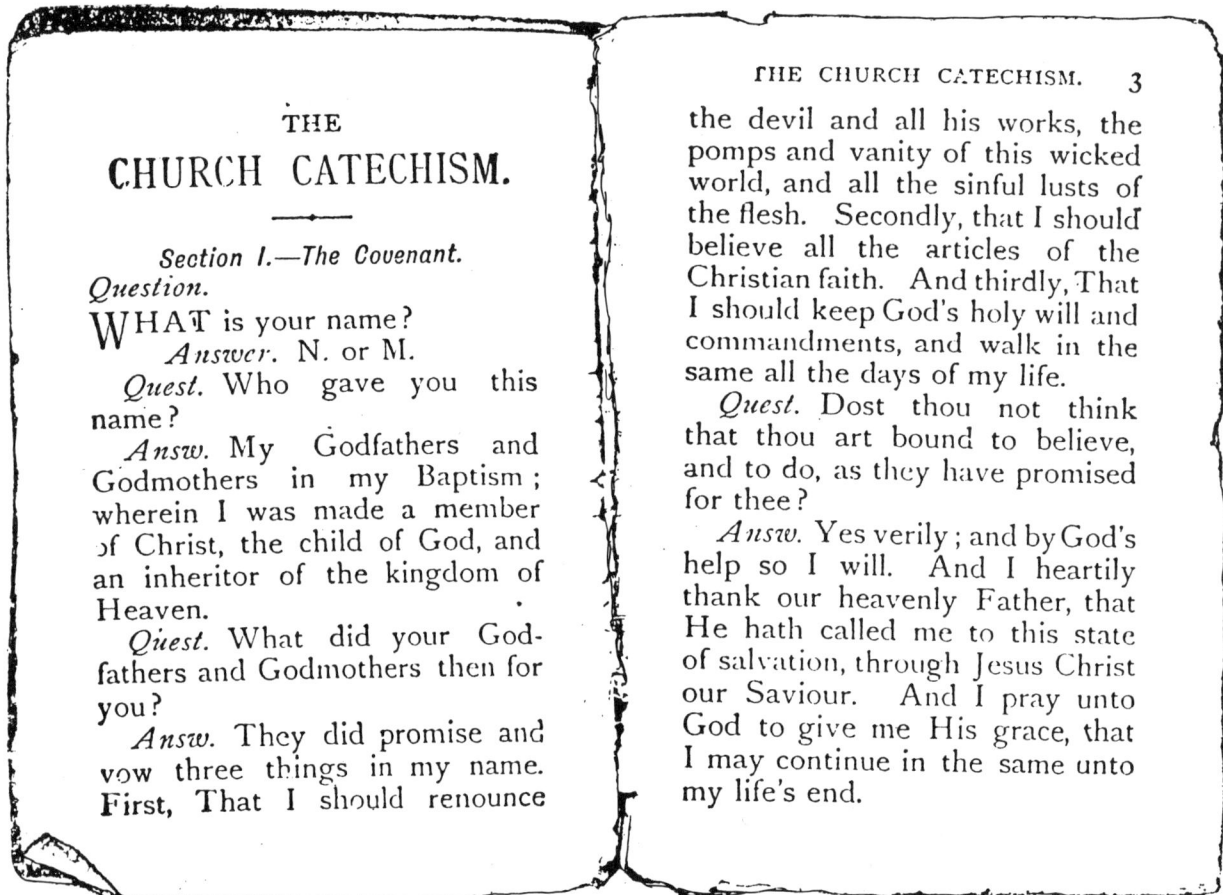

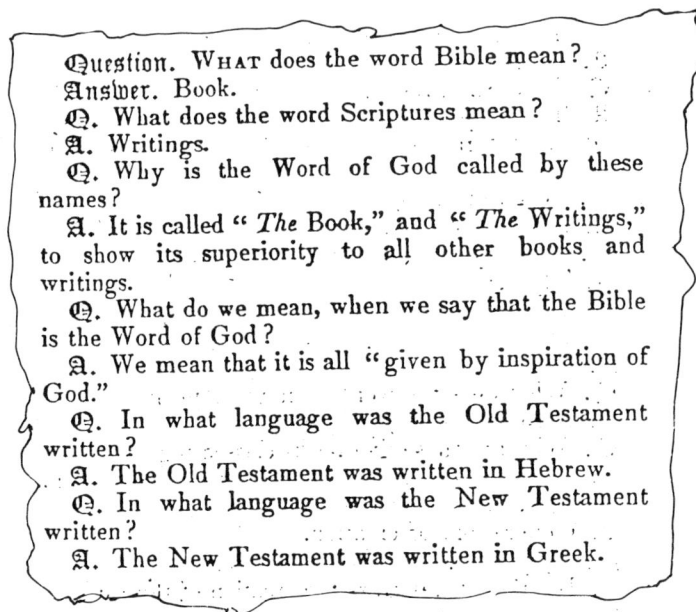

THE
# CHURCH CATECHISM.

Section I.—The Covenant.
*Question.*
WHAT is your name?
*Answer.* N. or M.
*Quest.* Who gave you this name?
*Answ.* My Godfathers and Godmothers in my Baptism; wherein I was made a member of Christ, the child of God, and an inheritor of the kingdom of Heaven.
*Quest.* What did your Godfathers and Godmothers then for you?
*Answ.* They did promise and vow three things in my name. First, That I should renounce

the devil and all his works, the pomps and vanity of this wicked world, and all the sinful lusts of the flesh. Secondly, that I should believe all the articles of the Christian faith. And thirdly, That I should keep God's holy will and commandments, and walk in the same all the days of my life.
*Quest.* Dost thou not think that thou art bound to believe, and to do, as they have promised for thee?
*Answ.* Yes verily; and by God's help so I will. And I heartily thank our heavenly Father, that He hath called me to this state of salvation, through Jesus Christ our Saviour. And I pray unto God to give me His grace, that I may continue in the same unto my life's end.

*Question.* WHAT does the word Bible mean?
*Answer.* Book.
*Q.* What does the word Scriptures mean?
*A.* Writings.
*Q.* Why is the Word of God called by these names?
*A.* It is called "*The* Book," and "*The* Writings," to show its superiority to all other books and writings.
*Q.* What do we mean, when we say that the Bible is the Word of God?
*A.* We mean that it is all "given by inspiration of God."
*Q.* In what language was the Old Testament written?
*A.* The Old Testament was written in Hebrew.
*Q.* In what language was the New Testament written?
*A.* The New Testament was written in Greek.

## THE ARK.

MORE than a thousand years passed away, and the world grew more and more wicked, so that God said that He would destroy mankind from the earth for their wickedness. But God is just and merciful, and would not destroy the good with the wicked. So He spoke to Noah, who was a good man, and told him that a great flood of water would come upon the earth, and would drown every man, and beast, and bird, and creeping thing. But God taught Noah how to build a large ship, called an ark, in which he might be saved from the flood.

Noah was rather more than five hundred years old when he was first ordered to make the ark, and he was six hundred years old when it was finished, so that there was time for the wicked people to have repented of their sins and turned to God. And when the ark was finished, God told Noah to enter it, and to take with him his wife, and his three sons, Shem, Ham, and Japhet, and their wives. And lest there should be no birds or beasts upon the earth, Noah was ordered to take into the ark seven pairs of all the beasts and birds which might be eaten or used for sacrifice, and one pair of all other creatures.

And when they had all passed into the ark, the rain began to fall from the clouds, and water rose out of the earth, and for forty days and forty nights the rain fell, and the waters rose, so that even the mountains were covered, and every living thing upon the earth was drowned in the water. But when the waters came to the place where the ark had been built, they lifted it up, and it floated upon the water, and all who were in it were saved.

For five months the water remained upon the earth, and all this while the ark floated about, as the wind blew it and the waves carried it. And when the five months had passed, God stopped the rain from falling, and allowed the water to run away into the earth, and in about six weeks the flood had fallen so much that the ark rested upon the top of a very high mountain called Ararat.

Still no land could be seen, and after Noah had waited forty days he sent a raven out of the ark. And the raven flew backwards and forwards, but did not return to the ark. So he sent a dove from the ark, and the dove found nothing to rest upon, and she came back again to Noah.

Then Noah waited for a week, and sent out the dove again, and in the evening the dove came back again with a fresh olive leaf in her mouth, so that Noah knew that the water had sunk low enough to allow the olive-trees to be seen. Now, the olive-trees are not tall trees, so that when the tops appeared above the water, Noah knew that the flood must be nearly gone.

But he waited for another week, and sent out the dove again, and this time she did not return, because she found trees on which she could rest, and leaves which she could eat. But Noah would not go out of the ark until God had told him to do so; and although he saw that the waters had gone away, and that the earth was dry, he waited in the ark.

And, after Noah and his family, and the birds, and the beasts, and the creeping things, had been shut up in the ark for more than a year, God told Noah to come out of the ark. And he came out, with all his family, and the beasts left the ark, and spread themselves over the world. And Noah took an ox, and a lamb, and a kid, and doves, and built an altar, and sacrificed them to God, and thanked Him for having saved them from the flood.

And God blessed Noah because he had obeyed His voice, and promised that He would never again send such a flood upon the earth. And God gave the rainbow as a pledge that He would keep His word, and told Noah that whenever men saw the rainbow, they were to remember that God had promised that mankind should never again be destroyed by a flood.

## Drill

Military type drill was the only exercise included in the school timetable and even then its main aim was not fitness but obedience. It was assumed that regular drill lessons would help discipline. In bad weather the pupils would have stood in the aisles between the desks to do drill, but you may find it easier if they stand at the desk. Alternatively, children could march to a suitable tune played on the piano.

*Drill exercises.*

Stand children in straight lines: heads up, shoulders back, feet together, hands by sides. Stand children an arm's width apart. The teacher counts. The class remains silent and copies the teacher's actions, synchronising movements. Repeat each exercise 4 times.

*Exercise 1*
1) Hands on shoulders. 2) Hands and arms straight above the head. 3) Hands on shoulders. 4) Hands by sides.

*Exercise 2*
1) Hands on shoulders. 2) Hands and arms straight out to the side. 3) Hands on shoulders 4) Hands by sides.

*Exercise 3*
1) Hands on shoulders 2) Hands and arms straight out to the front 3) Hands and arms straight out to the sides 4) Hands by sides

*Exercise 4: Touching the toes*
1) Hands and arms straight out ot the front 2) Bend to touch the toes without bending the knees 3) Rise, hands out in front. 4) Hands by sides.

*Exercise 5: Marching on the spot*
1) Lift up left leg. Lower. 2) Lift up right leg. Lower. 3) Lift up left leg and right arm. Lower. 4) Lift up right leg and left arm. Lower. 5) Lift up left leg and right arm. Now march on the spot in time: *'Left, right, left, right. Heads up, shoulders back'*. March for a suitable length of time. Command: *'Class stop'*.
(If in the classroom): *'Class sit'*.

...'J.G.Fitch Esq., H.M.Inspector of Training Colleges, having kindly suggested to the author that a course of Musical Drill, which could be utilized indoors, would prove both useful and beneficial - when, owing to inclement weather or other cause, the children would have been confined to the schoolroom at their desks - I have arranged the following exercises for that purpose. All the movements will be found to be practicable at close quarters'.

*Exercise 1*

i)      Stand to attention with hands at the sides
ii)     Bring your hands clenched to your chest
iii)    Reach up above your head
iv)     Back to original position at attention

*Exercise 2*

i)      Place your hands on your waist with fingers pointing forward
ii)     Turn your head to the right
iii)    To the front
iv)     To the left
v)      To the front
vi)     Backwards
vii)    Back to the front again

*Exercise 3*

i)      Place your hands on your waist, this time with thumbs pointing forward
ii)     Pull your elbows back
iii)    Push them back to the original position

*Exercise 4*

i)      Place your hands on your waist with fingers to the front
ii)     Turn from the waist to the right
iii)    To the left
iv)     Back to the front

*Exercise 5*

i)      Mark time by lifting your left and then your right foot alternately from the floor
ii)     Bring your right knee up and let it drop back to the floor
iii)    Repeat with the left knee

**History**

A lesson can be based on a portrait of Queen Victoria. Explain how she came to the throne in 1837 when only 18 and how God has helped her, over the years, to bear her duties and responsibilities as queen, wife and mother. In the same way everyone, however humble, should look to God for guidance and should take the queen as a shining example.

This gives an opportunity to mention Prince Albert and possibly to look at a family tree and to find the names of the royal children. You could reminisce about the Golden Jubilee and pray that God will spare Her Majesty for many years to come.

Read out the enclosed passage and ask questions about it.

VICTORIA BECOMES QUEEN, 1837.

William IV left no children. The heir to the throne was his niece, Victoria, the child of his brother the Duke of Kent. The Princess Victoria had been brought up most carefully by her mother, the Duchess of Kent. The Duchess felt it to be her first duty rightly to prepare her child for the great post which she would one day have to fill. They lived together very quietly in Kensington Palace, away from all the bustle and the gaiety of the Court. There one morning early Victoria, then only eighteen years old, was awakened to be told that messengers were come from Windsor with the news that the King was dead. Hastily throwing a shawl over her nightdress, she received the Prime Minister, Lord Melbourne, who came to greet her as his Queen. A few hours afterwards the young Queen had to meet her Council. Pale and calm, she took her seat at the head of the table, and spoke a few simple words, in which she showed her earnest wish to do what was for the good of her people. Every one was charmed with her behaviour, which gave them good hope that she would really be a blessing to her people.

The next day she showed herself dressed simply in black at the window of St. James' Palace to the people, and wept when their shouts of joy filled the air. The hopes which filled men's hearts that day have not been disappointed. She has made herself the head of the people, has felt with them and for them, and has been willing to govern according to their wishes.

(from 'A First History of England' by L. Creighton. 1881)

QUEEN VICTORIA'S FIRST COUNCIL.

40

Please note that the Royal family tree, a map of the Empire and an A3 size outline of the Union Jack are contained in the (optional) accompanying Resource Folder. You could use the map of the Empire to talk about British possessions and the status of the queen as its ruler. Here is an elderly person's memory of Empire Day which, in 1897, was fixed to be celebrated on May 24th:

> 'Empire Day was another day to remember. Britannia presided over a group of children dressed in the National costume of the countries of the Empire. Verse speaking, singing and a colourful pageant were performed before an audience of doting parents and local dignitaries. We danced around the maypole, drank lemonade and ate sticky buns. Our patriotic fervour was only second to our delight at having a half day's holiday for the occasion'.

Children could make a Union Flag, e.g. colour in the outline, and learn about the saints using this poem. You could have large card cut-outs to hold up whilst you are explaining it.

### THE UNION JACK

This little flag to us so dear,
The Union Jack of fame,
Come, sit by me, and you shall hear
The way it got its name.

We first must look at other three,
Please hold them up quite tight,
They all have crosses, you can see,
Two red ones and one white.

St. Patrick's Cross, to Ireland dear,
Like letter X it lies;
St. George's Cross so bright and clear,
Led England's battle cries.

St Andrew's Cross is white, you see,
Upon a bed of blue,
The Scottish flag it used to be,
To it the folks were true.

In course of time, the three combin'd,
It was a famous tack:
We'll do the same, and you will find,
Great Britain's Union Jack.

There would have been a picture of Queen Victoria in many homes and classrooms, as patriotism was very much alive. The Union Jack would appear, and the National Anthem be sung on every suitable occasion, including the birthdays of all members of the royal family. Here is a list in case you wish to implement this custom and happen to be holding your schoolday on one of these dates.

*Dates that could be celebrated:*

| | |
|---|---|
| Marriage of Queen Victoria and Prince Albert | 10th February, 1840 |
| St. David's day | 1st March |
| St. Patrick's day | 17th March |
| Birth of 6th child, Princess Louise | 18th March, 1848 |
| Birth of 8th child, Prince Leopold | 7th April, 1853 |
| Birth of 9th child, Princess Beatrice | 14th April, 1857 |
| St. George's day | 23rd April |
| Birth of 3rd child, Princess Alice | 25th April, 1843 |
| Birth of 7th child, Prince Arthur | 1st May, 1850 |
| Marriage of Prince of Wales to Princess Alexandra | 10th May. 1863 |
| Birth of Queen Victoria | 24th May, 1819 |
| Birth of 5th child, Princess Helena | 25th May, 1846 |
| Accession of Queen Victoria | 20th June, 1837 |
| Queen Victoria's Silver Jubilee | 20th June, 1862 |
| Queen Victoria's Golden Jubilee | 20th June, 1887 |
| Queen Victoria's Diamond Jubilee | 20th June, 1897 |
| Coronation of Queen Victoria | 28th June, 1838 |
| Birth of Prince Albert | 26th August, 1819 |
| Birth of 4th child, Prince Alfred | 26th August, 1844 |
| Birth of 2nd child, Prince Albert Edward, the heir | 9th November, 1841 |
| Birth of 1st child, Princess Victoria | 21st November, 1840 |
| St. Andrew's day | 30th November |

*Deaths:*

Prince Albert died on 14th December, 1861
Princess Alice died on 14th December, 1878
Prince Leopold died on 28th March, 1884
Prince Alfred died on 31st July, 1900
Queen Victoria died on 22nd January, 1901

*The Church calendar:*

This was observed strictly and days such as Ascension Day and Advent would have been celebrated in school.

This is a page from a child's history book, published in 1885. (Reproduction copies of 'The Historical House that Jack Built' can be obtained from Sevington School).

HENRY VII

Born 1456, began to reign 1485.

This is HENRY THE SEVENTH, of *Tudor* line ;
Two insurrections disturb'd his reign,
But courage and vigilance made them vain.
His policy much the realm improv'd,
Though hoarding his money he dearly lov'd.
He won the great battle of Bosworth field,
Where Richard the Third in fight was kill'd, &c.

HENRY VIII.

Born 1492, began to reign 1509.

This is HENRY THE EIGHTH, who married six wives,
And ended by violence two of their lives :
He was a tyrant, fat, savage, and proud ;
Yet still he was useful, it must be allow'd,
As first of the sov'reigns who govern'd this nation,
That sanction'd the Protestant Reformation,
Crown'd in the year *Fifteen hundred and nine,*
Son of Henry the Seventh, of Tudor line, &c.

EDWARD VI.

Born 1537, began to reign 1547.

The next that rul'd was that excellent youth,
A pattern of piety, wisdom, and truth,
King EDWARD THE SIXTH, who left this sad scene
For the regions of bliss at the age of sixteen.
Son of Henry the Eighth, who married six wives, &c.

MARY.

Born 1516, began to reign 1553.

This is MARY, that married KING PHILIP OF SPAIN,
(May times such as hers be ne'er seen again,)
Full of " zeal without knowledge," she Protestants burn'd,
Unless to the Romish religion they turn'd.
*Cranmer, Ridley,* and *Latimer* perish'd in flames,
And distant posterity honours their names.
Half-sister was she to that excellent youth, &c.

Famous stories from history might be told:

Ten hundred years ago there was a king of England who had a son, whose name was Alfred. When the young prince was twelve years of age, he had not learned to read.

In those days there were few men or women that could read or write.

Now Alfred's mother was able to read. One day she was sitting with a book in her hand, and Alfred and his brothers were standing around her. The book had a great many pretty pictures in it, and the boys were very fond of looking at them.

Their mother wished that the boys should learn to read, so she said that she would give the book with the pretty pictures to the one who should learn to read first. Alfred took great pains to learn, and he was soon able to read the whole of the book to his mother. His mother then gave Alfred the book to himself, and you may be sure that he was very proud of his prize.

After this Alfred learned to write. He also got by heart the songs which old men called minstrels sang and played on the harp. He sang these songs to his mother, who loved to hear him sing and play.

When Alfred grew up to be a man, he became king of England. He was so wise and did so much good to the land, that he has ever since been called Alfred the Great.

**Geography**

This often meant learning a lot of facts by heart e.g. the names of the rivers of England working down the coast from north to south. Such rote-learning did not foster independent thought nor any real understanding.

However, A.H.Garlick in 'A New Manual of Method' suggests a more enterprising approach to geography lessons. Here pupils could read the passage below about the River Thames, learn the vocabulary and then answer questions.

Pupils could also learn the points of the compass and other facts about Britain and the world.

## RIVERS.

The chief points to be noticed in giving a lesson on rivers are here enumerated, but it is not suggested that *every* lesson should contain all the information specified. The time allowed and the class must be the chief determining factors. The points should always be introduced in the order recommended, so as to preserve the proper sequence in teaching—from the more known to the less known. Children may see a river day by day, and may also see its various uses exemplified. They probably know little or nothing about its formation, and therefore this should generally come last. We will take the Thames as an example.

1. Uses.—It is a great *commercial highway* ; ships laden with goods from all parts of the world pass up and down it continually. Many *trades* are carried on along its banks, whilst with its steamboats it affords a pleasant means of *communication* between one place and another. It contributes to the *water supply* of the people, for some companies draw largely from it ; whilst the fish caught at its mouth and in its upper courses increase the *food supply*. In its prettier parts it is even used as a *residential place*, for many house boats are now found upon it. It also affords opportunities for swimming, rowing, sailing, punting, and fishing, while pleasure parties by steam boats or rowing boats swarm upon it. These facts show its *recreative* use to be one of the most important.

2. Course.—Follow the course from its source to its mouth, and take the opportunity to teach right and left banks, shore, bed, channel, tributary, mouth, course, basin, estuary, chief towns, bridges, tunnels, and chief ferries.

3. Formation.—Describe the circulation of water on the globe—evaporation, condensation, atmospheric phenomena (rain, snow, etc.), the percolation of rain, and the formation of springs. For other rivers it may be necessary to describe the formation of a glacier, and to show that some rivers take their rise from them.

## HOW TO TEACH THE POINTS OF THE COMPASS.

**1. Fix the South.**—Wait for a suitable day, and then turn to the sun at mid-day. Explain south as meaning the sun quarter, and from this find all the other cardinal points in the following order: N., E., and W. Do *not* start with the N.

**2. Fix the Directions in the Schoolroom.**—Mark them, with their initials, on the floor or walls. In London Board schools they are painted on the ceiling. In Glasgow they are fixed by means of brass bars inserted in the granolite at the school threshold.

**3. North.**—Show how the top of the map is N. To do this lay the B.B. on the floor, and mark there the true directions thus found. Then place the B.B. on an easel, and show how N. comes to be at the top, but explain that N. does not mean up higher than the rest; that the existing arrangement is merely one of convenience.

**4. Other Points.**—Explain the principle of naming the other points. Describe each by means of the two bounding it; *e.g.*, N.E. means some spot between the N. and the E. It is both N. and E., and is therefore said to be N.E. So with the other points, N.W., S.W., and S.E. Then proceed to finer differences such as W.N.W.; *i.e.*, between W. and N.W. In this way work out all the points of the compass.

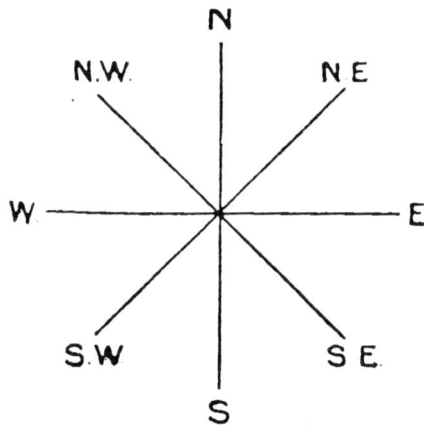

**5. Compass.**—The compass itself should now be introduced to the class. Explain the word compass by showing that its points *compass the circle*, and the earth is circular in shape. The class will then see why its points are called points of the compass. Deviation and the magnetic qualities of the compass should form a later lesson. A "model" compass might be built by the teacher in front of the class, and with a little preparation and ingenuity each child might also make one at the same time.

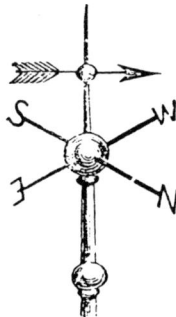

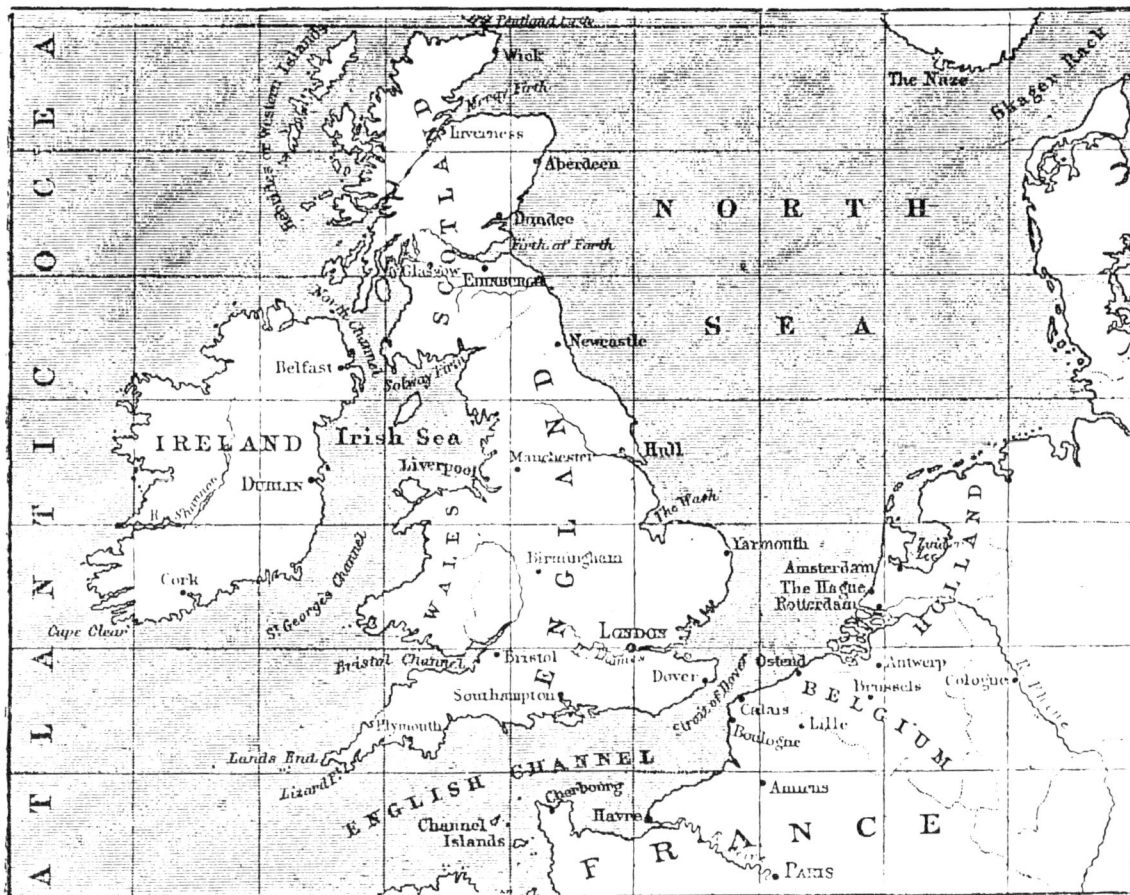

## OUR ISLAND HOME.

1. Here is a map of the **British Isles.** They consist of two large islands, (Great Britain and Ireland,) and a number of small islands.

2. The British Isles lie on the north-west of Europe, in the Atlantic Ocean. The North Sea on the east and the English Channel on the south separate those islands from the Continent.

3. Great Britain, the larger of the two islands, consists of England, Wales, and Scotland.

4. Great Britain is the largest island in Europe. It is the seventh island in size among the islands of the globe.

5. This is what we call " Our Island Home." It is one of the smallest and yet one of the most powerful countries in the world.

6. Our Queen rules over other parts of the world. The whole of her dominions is called the British Empire. It includes one-seventh part of the land surface of the globe.

7. London, the capital of England, is the largest and wealthiest city in the world.

7. A map of the world is sometimes drawn on a large ball called a globe. This globe is fixed in a frame, and

looks like a little world. If you turn it round, you will see first the one side and then the other.

6. Make a square. Let the square stand for the Earth's surface. Divide it into quarters. Mark one quarter land and the other three water. This will

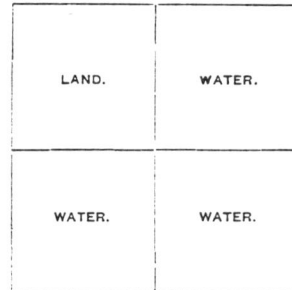

| LAND. | WATER. |
|-------|--------|
| WATER. | WATER. |

remind you that there is three times as much water as there is land on the surface of the globe.

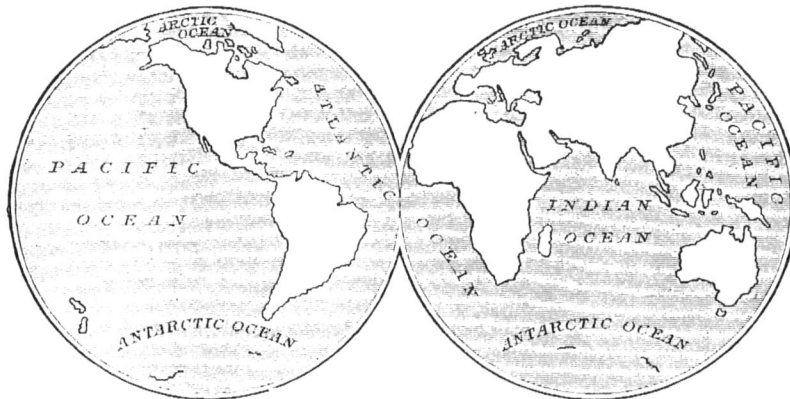

## THE SIZE OF THE EARTH.

1. The Earth is a large ball—so very large that there is nothing we have ever seen to which we can compare it.

2. Men of science have measured it, and they tell us that the circumference, or distance round it, is about 25,000 miles; and that the diameter, or distance through it, is about 8000 miles.

3. These figures show us that the Earth is very large; but from them we can hardly form an idea of its great size.

4. From the one end of England to the other the distance is about 400 miles. Walking at the rate of three miles an hour, for ten hours a day, we should spend thirteen days on this journey.

5. But England is only a very small part of the whole Earth. To make a journey equal to the distance round the Earth, we should have to walk from the one end of England to the other nearly sixty-three times.

6. Suppose that some morning we were to say "Good-bye" to our friends and start on such a journey, we should be from home nearly three years.

7. If the Earth were all land, the fastest railway train, travelling night and day, would take a month to go round it.

8. To find out exactly the meaning of the words circumference and diameter, get an orange, and measure round the widest part of it: that is its circumference. Cut it into two equal parts, and then measure across the middle of one of the flat faces: that is its diameter.

9. The circumference is about three times the diameter. If the orange measure nine inches round the outside, it will measure about three inches from side to side through the centre.

REMEMBER:—**The Circumference of the Earth is about 25,000 miles. The Diameter of the Earth is about 8000 miles.**

**The Object Lesson**

This was often considered suitable practice for the pupil teacher. It was particularly popular with infant classes and might include such diverse things as bread, paper, an orange, Roman numerals or the potato and the apple as in these examples:

*The Potato*

Give each pair of pupils a potato. Get them to describe the colour, the feel, the smell, the shape etc. Then use the following questions and answers. (The question and answer method was a common teaching technique based on memory.)

### The Training of the Senses.

One of the primary objects of object teaching is the proper training of the senses, especially of sight and touch, which are pre-eminently the intellectual senses. The importance of sense training is further recognised by the admission of hand and eye training, kindergarten and its developments, drawing, clay modelling, and manual instruction into the school curriculum. All these exercise the senses in a number of ways, and so supply the materials of knowledge; for there can be neither a wide nor an accurate knowledge of the world around us without *the proper exercise of the senses through material objects*. This is the first and most important element in the training of the senses.

### POTATO

Q.  Is not the potato one of the most useful roots we possess?

A.  Yes; it forms the principal food of many of the poor in this country, and in Ireland they chiefly live upon it.

Q.  To what country are we indebted for such a valuable plant ?

A.  It has been said that Sir Francis Drake first brought it from Santa Fe, in New Mexico, North America.

Q.  But what great man is said to have first planted it in Ireland ?

A.  Sir Walter Raleigh, at Youghal, in the county of Cork, in the reign of James I.

Q.  What county in England is thought to excel in this vegetable ?

A.  Lancashire; Formby, a few miles north of Liverpool, is remarkable for producing the best in the country.

Q.  What old story is related with regard to this ?

A.  It is said that a vessel laden with potatoes from Ireland to London, was driven on shore at Formby, which occasioned them to be first planted at that place.

Q.  Was not their progress very slow ?

A.  Yes; they were for a long time only grown as delicacies in the gardens of men of fortune, and even in the time of Charles I they are named as articles provided for the Queen's table, at the price of two shillings per pound.

**Science**

It would not be feasible to set up a Victorian Science lesson so we suggest that, if it is to be included, you present it as a botany or simple biology object lesson. You might examine deciduous and evergreen leaves, twigs and buds, the garden snail or the earthworm.

*The Apple*

Give each pair of children half an apple cut longitudinally. The teacher should also have another apple cut transversely.
On the blackboard, draw both the transverse and the longitudinal sections and label them.
Alternatively you could prepare A3 size charts, in advance, by enlarging this diagram.
Discuss with the pupils the purpose of the fruit of a plant (which contains the seeds).
Ask them for the names of other fruits (not recent imports).
Point to each labelled part of the fruit. Say the name and ask the children to repeat it. Use a pointer for this.
Hold up the transverse half and discuss the shape of the seed compartment in the centre, the shape of the apple. the skin, the stalk etc.
Ask the children to draw the longitudinal half on their slates or on paper and to label it neatly, using the proper names.

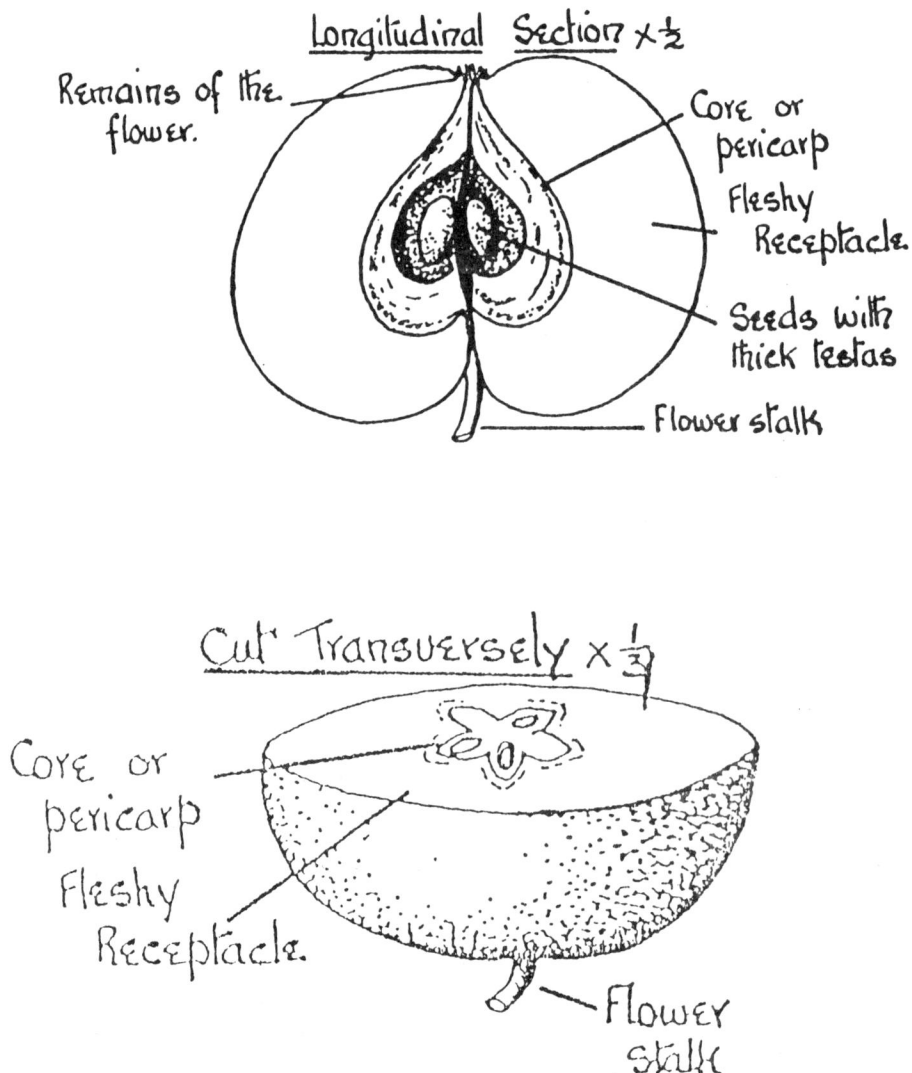

Longitudinal Section x ½

Remains of the flower.

Core or pericarp

Fleshy Receptacle.

Seeds with thick testas

Flower stalk

Cut Transversely x ½

Core or pericarp

Fleshy Receptacle.

Flower stalk

## Drawing

Geometric drawing was often taught to the boys whilst the girls did needlework. It was very mechanical and did not demand any imagination. Sometimes the pupils would copy diagrams like the ones below, or draw models of cubes, cones and cylinders (solid wooden shapes, painted light grey). Occasionally, they drew a single flower, or a small branch with leaves.

Exercise I

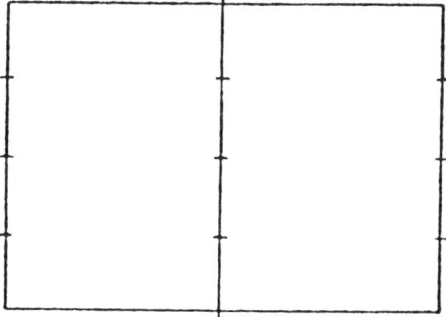

A.

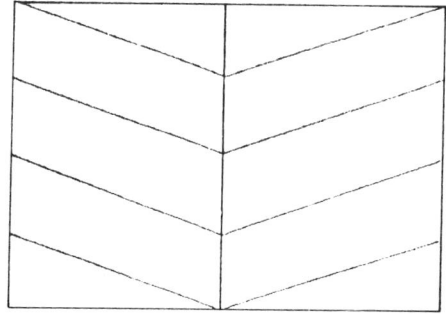

B.

Exercise II

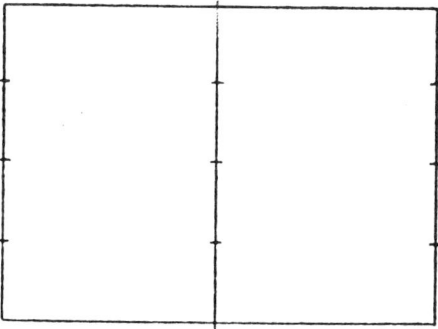

A.

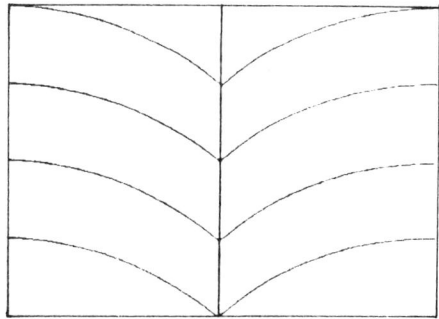

B.

Exercise III

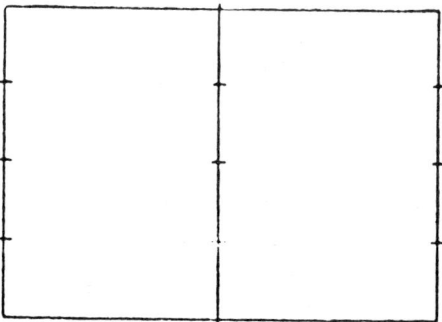

A.

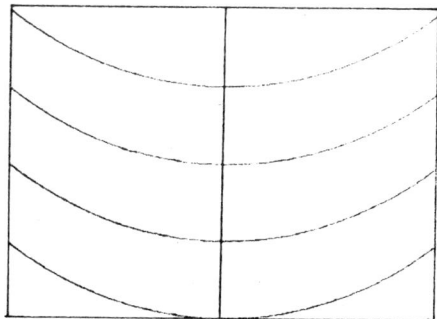

B.

**Sewing**

This was only taught to the girls. It was a very important subject since very few people could afford one of the new sewing machines, introduced into England in 1846. In 1870 the cost was 6 guineas whereas the wage of a farm labourer was only about 10/-.

This meant that the mother of a family had to make or mend most of her children's clothes by hand. (Mass-produced garments were not readily available until the very end of the 19th century.) A girl going into domestic service would be expected to repair the linen neatly. Also taking in sewing could often supplement a meagre income.

The girls would be given a piece of calico with some coloured cotton and they would have to practice tiny, regular running stitches. Later they might make a sampler to demonstrate different stitches. They would also practise sewing on buttons, making button holes, patching and darning. By the time they were 7 or 8 many of them would be proficient needlewomen, able to start making garments such as chemises and nightgowns, all by hand. You could add some interest by arranging for the needlework to be inspected by the vicar's wife or daughter who would often have taken a personal interest in the girls' progress. Remember that persons of such eminent social standing would have beem treated with great deference and this should be reflected in the role-play.

This is an opportunity to bring in phrases like *a stitch in time saves nine*. Also don't forget to use thimbles - another authentic touch.

N.B. A practicality worth noting - it is not a good idea to timetable sewing immediately after writing with pen and ink.

In this etching, notice the tiered gallery, the gas light and the bare walls.

*Reproduced from the Archive of the History of Education at Leeds University*

## ROSE COOPER'S SAMPLER

This small apron was made by an 11-year-old girl who practised the following types of stitches:

1  Hemming

2  Gathering

3  Buttonholes

4  Eyelet holes

5  Loops

6  Sewing on a button

7  Sewing on tape

8  Pleats

9  Patch

10 Herring bone stitch

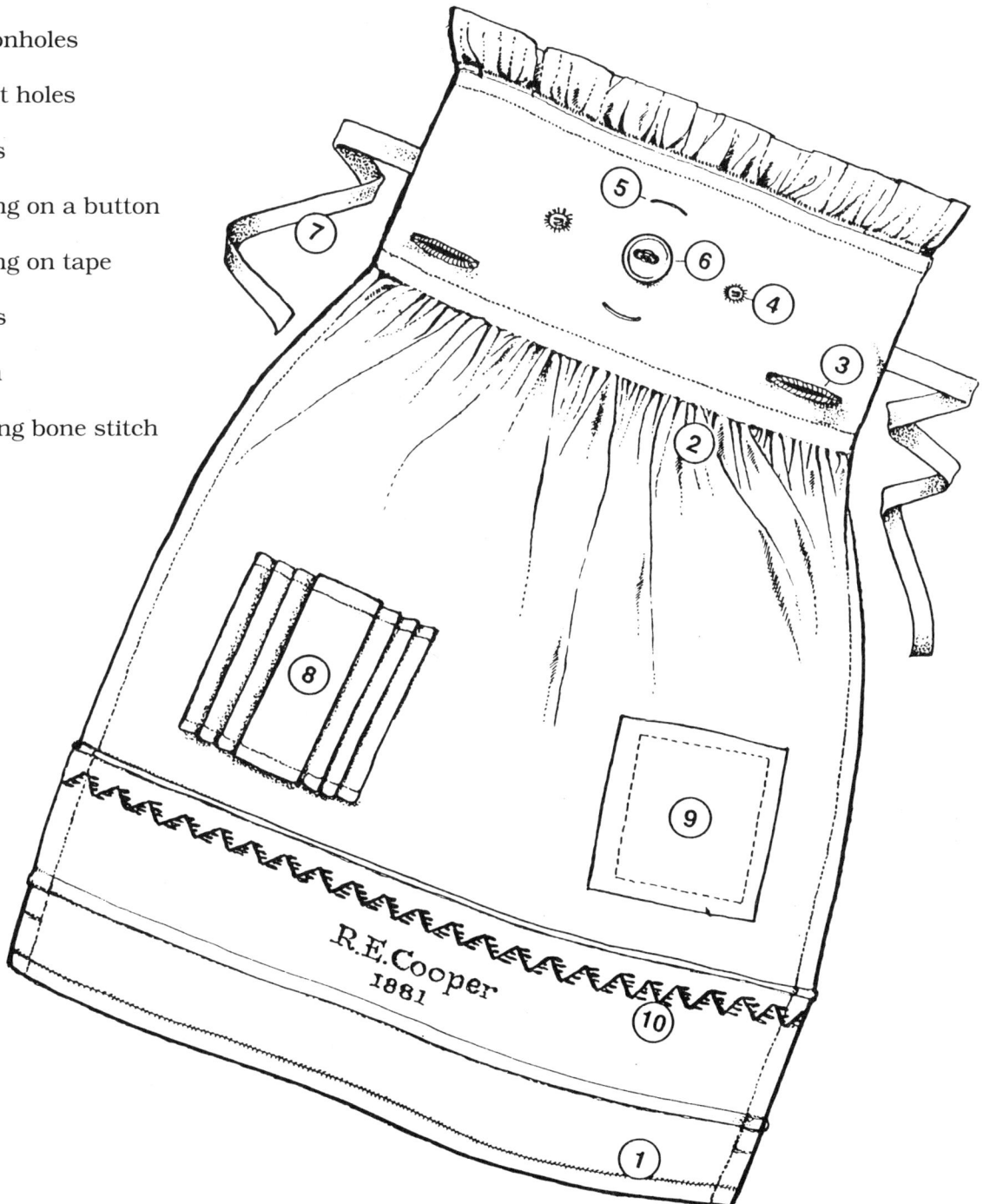

*Reproduced from 'Victorian Times' - Jo Lawrie and Paul Noble, Collins Educational.*

Most of these stitches are unlikely to be familiar to today's pupil and might be too difficult. You could let the girls try sewing on a tape or button or stitching a name on a bookmark.

ABCDEFGHIJKLM
NOPQRSTUVWXY
Z.123456789101112
abcdefghijklmnopq
rstuvwxyz.131415

Remember now thy
Creator
Thou God seest me

Priscilla Pearce
Sevington School
1874

**A Moral Tale**

This could be read aloud to the children whilst they are sewing or drawing.

'TRUE DUNCAN'

6. There was once a little boy named Duncan. The boys used to call him "True Duncan," because he would never tell a lie. One day he was playing with an axe in the school-yard. The axe was used for cutting wood for the school-room fire in winter.

7. While Duncan was chopping a stick, the teacher's cat, Old Tabby, came and leaped on to the log of wood where Duncan was at work. He had raised the axe to cut the wood, but it fell on the cat and killed her. What to do he knew not. She was the master's pet, and used to sit on a cushion at his side while he was hearing the boys their lessons.

8. Duncan stood looking at poor Tabby. His face grew red, and the tears stood in his eyes. All the boys came running up, and every one had something to say. One of them was heard whispering to the others, "Now, boys, let us see if Duncan can't make up a fib as well as the rest of us."—"Not he," said Tom Brown, who was Duncan's friend, "not he; I'll warrant Duncan will be true as gold."

9. John Jones stepped up and said, "Come, boys; let us fling the cat into the lane, and we can tell Mr. Cole that the butcher's dog killed her. You know that he worried her last week." Some of them thought that that would do very well. But Duncan looked quite angry. His cheeks swelled, and his face grew redder than before. "No! no!" said he. "Do you think I would say that? It would be a *lie*—a LIE!" Each time he used the word his voice grew louder.

10. Then he took up the poor thing and carried her into the school-room. The boys followed, to see what would happen. The master looked up and said, "What is this? my poor Tabby killed? Who could have done me such an injury?"

11. All were silent for a little while. As soon as Duncan could get his voice, he said, "Mr. Cole, I am very sorry. I killed poor Tabby. Indeed, sir, I am *very* sorry. I ought to have been more careful, for I saw her rubbing herself against the log. I am more sorry than I can tell, sir."

12. Every one expected to see Mr. Cole get very angry, take down his cane, and give Duncan a sound thrashing. But instead of that, he put on a pleasant smile and said, "Duncan, you are a brave boy! I saw and heard all that passed in the yard, from my window above. I am glad to see such an example of truth and honour in my school."

13. Duncan took out his handkerchief and wiped his eyes. The boys couldn't keep silence any longer; and when Tom Brown cried, "Three cheers for True Duncan," they all joined, and made the school-house ring with a hearty hurrah.

14. The teacher then said, "My boys, I am glad you know what is right, and that you approve it; though I am afraid some of you could not have done it. Learn from this time that nothing can make a lie necessary. Suppose Duncan had taken your evil advice, and come to me with a lie: it would have been instantly detected, and instead of the honour of truth, he would have had only the shame of falsehood." ____

**Singing**

Most schools did not have a piano so the teacher sang the first note or used a tuning fork. You could practise hymns, the National Anthem or suitable patriotic songs such as 'Here's a Health unto Her Majesty', 'Rule Britannia'.

## IV.—VOCAL GYMNASTICS: EXERCISES IN CORRECT ARTICULATION.

These exercises are designed to teach children to avoid slovenly habits of pronunciation, to speak clearly and distinctly, and to improve recitation and reading.

### Set A.—INITIAL CONSONANTS.

#### Double and Difficult.

*th-* (1) *three, thrive, thrushes, thrash, thresh, thrill, throttle, thread, thirty, through.*

(2) *Illustrative sentences:*
   i. thirty three thousand thrushes thrive.
   ii. thrust thread through thick cloth.
   iii. thrust thick thorns through the three thieves' throats.
   iv. thwart thoughtless thieves?

*sh-* (1) *sheep, shrink, shrill, shells, shower, shiver, shroud, shred, shrine.*

(2) *Illustrative sentences:*
   sheep shiver in the shower.
   shrink the cloth.      shrill notes were heard.
   she sells sea-shells.      she sells shell fish.
   shrouded in mist.      shells and shingle.
   a shapely sash should not show shabby stitches.

### Set B.—SOUND OF "R."

*r-* (soft sound)   bar, arm, earth, father.

*rr-* (trilled)   (1) *red, rid, rod, rude, rare, shrill, thrill, thrilled, row, round, roaring, roll, road, bran, broad. rattle, wriggle.*

(2) *Illustrative sentences:*
   i. around the rugged rocks the ragged rascal ran.
   ii. row, brothers, row against the roaring river.
   iii. rats ran right across the rusty rails.
   iv. roll, roller, roll across the rugged road.

### Set C.—FINAL CONSONANTS.

*Note.—Bite at these firmly.*

*-t* (1) kept, pept, slept, wept, crept, sweet, night, light, act, mast, trust.

*-sts* (2) fists, mists, posts, nests, thrusts, thirsts, lists, ghosts. hosts, toasts, masts, bursts.

(3) *Illustrative sentences for frequent repetition:*
   i. he crept into bed, but wept before he slept.
   ii. a light at the mast head.      lost sheep.
   iii. light came next night through the mists.
   iv. he thrusts his fists against the posts.
   v. the wasps' nests were difficult to catch.
   vi. went out into the harvest field.
   vii. what are the lengths of the masts?

**Poetry**

Learning poems by heart was considered to be an important part of a child's education.  It was thought to give pupils confidence and control of vocal delivery as well as cultivating taste and imagination, even if they were poor readers.

Some suitable ones are:

| | |
|---|---|
| 'I remember, I remember' | Thomas Hood |
| 'The Song of the Shirt' | Thomas Hood |
| 'The Village Blacksmith' | H.W.Longfellow |
| 'Hiawatha's Childhood' | H.W.Longfellow |
| 'The Lamplighter' | R.L.Stevenson |
| 'The Brook' | Lord Tennyson |
| 'The Charge of the Light Brigade' | Lord Tennyson |
| 'The Daffodils' | W. Wordsworth |

Pupils could be required to learn part of a poem by rote and then recite it to the rest of the class.

PLAYING AT HORSES.

1. When school is over and lessons are done,
   Off for a scamper the children run.
 " Harry and Sam, and Mary and Fan,
   You shall be horses ; I'll be the man."

2. So said Freddy, the youngest of all ;
   The children at once all ran to his call.
   A cord for the rein, but no whip had he ;
   They galloped away when he cried, " Gee ! "

3. Playing at horses, when work is all done,
   The children think is the best of fun ;
   Often they go to the tree in the lane,
   Right through the garden, and home again.

———————

# Three Green Bonnets

### 1.

Three green bonnets at church one day,
Dulcie and Daisy and Dorothy-May;
Three green bonnets that sat in a row,
Each bonnet tied with a green ribbon bow;
One pair of blue eyes and one pair of grey,
And one pair of brown eyes, that's Dorothy-May.

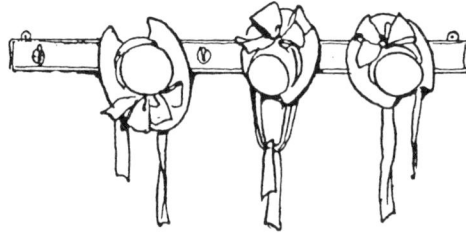

### 2.

Three little heads at the close of day,
Dulcie and Daisy and Dorothy-May;
Three little heads of clustering curls,
Three little beds and three little girls;
The blue eyes are weeping, and so are the grey,
For Angels are peeping at Dorothy-May.

### 3.

Three green bonnets have had their day,
Dulcie and Daisy and Dorothy-May;
Three green bonnets grown old unawares,
Hang on the pegs at the foot of the stairs;
And blue eyes are swollen and so are the grey,
For angels have stolen dear Dorothy-May.

## Poisonous Fruit 〜 〜 〜

AS Tommy and his sister Jane
 Were walking down a shady lane,
They saw some berries, bright and red,
That hung around and over head;

And soon the bough they bended down,
To make the scarlet fruit their own;
And part they ate, and part, in play,
They threw about, and flung away.

But long they had not been at home
Before poor Jane and little Tom
Were taken sick, and ill, to bed,
And since, I've heard, they both are dead.

Alas! had Tommy understood
That fruit in lanes is seldom good,
He might have walked with little Jane
Again along the shady lane.

## Playing with Fire 〜 〜

THE friends of little Mary Green
 Are now in deep distress,
The family will soon be seen
 To wear a mournful dress!

It seems from litter on the floor,
 She had been lighting straws,
Which caught the muslin frock she wore,
 A sad event to cause.

Her screams were loud and quickly heard,
 And remedies applied,
But all in vain, she scarcely stirr'd
 Again, before she died!

## A VISIT BY THE INSPECTOR

This would be awaited with fear and trepidation, not least because the results affected the teachers' salaries.

An inspector's comments.

*Inspected July 28th 1897.*

*In this little School of eleven children a sufficient amount of Scripture was presented.*

*These children were somewhat shy & reticent but the rest answered freely and knew their work well.*

*An exceptionally large quantity of repetition was known, both of Scripture and of Hymns, and the elder children answered nicely in Prayer Book and Catechism.*

*The behaviour was excellent.*

*Charles J. Parker.*

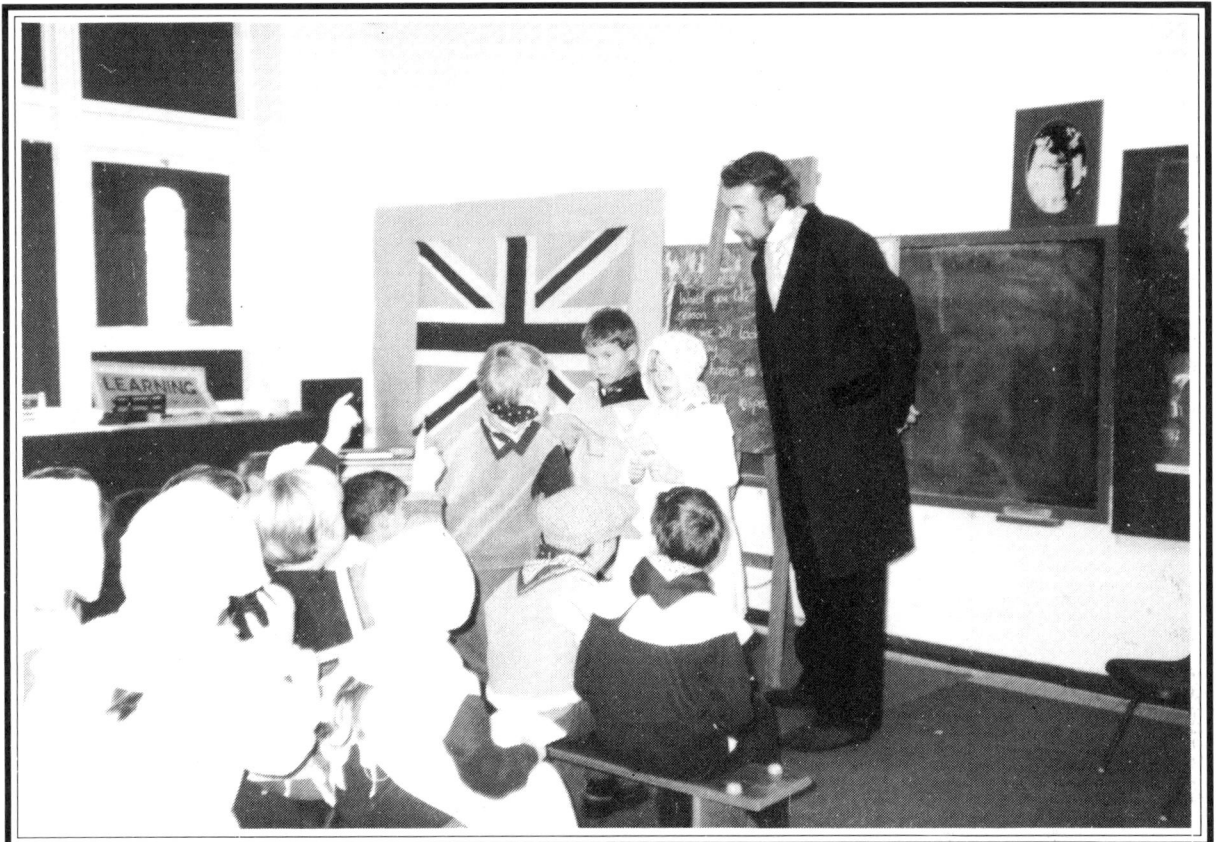

## PRESENTATION OF CERTIFICATES AND MEDALS

At the end of the day you could give out attendance certificates and medals or merit certificates. The school inspector could be invited to look at the children's work and then make the presentation. Here is an original certificate for you to photocopy. (You could make your own medal on a card and affix a ribbon and a pin.)

### CERTIFICATE OF MERIT

PRESENTED TO

..........................................

aged ............ years, who, having attended this School during the preceding year, passed in the ............ Standard at the Examination held by Her Majesty's Inspector on the ............ day of ............ 18 ....

Signed ............................

*Pardon, O Lord, I beseech Thee, those sins I have committed
against Thy Divine Majesty this day; and by Thy great mercy
defend me from all the perils and dangers of this night,
for the love of Thy only Son, our Saviour Jesus Christ.*
*Amen.*

*I Thank Thee, O Heavenly Father, for Thy care over me during
the past day. Watch over me this night and make me dwell
in safety. Forgive the sins of which I have been guilty.
Help me to grow in Thy faith and fear. Make me to love
Thee with all my heart, and soul, and mind, and strength.
Bless my father and mother, and all people,
and hear my prayer, for Jesus Christ's sake.*
*Amen.*

*Lord keep us safe this night
Secure from all our fears
May Angels guard us while we sleep
'Till morning light appears.*
*Amen.*

N.B. Once again, specifically Christian references may be excluded if necessary for a multi-
ethnic class.

# APPENDICES

# APPENDICES

## APPENDIX I:   EDUCATION 1762 - 1902 (an outline for the teacher).

1762 Jean Jacques Rousseau published his liberal ideas on education in 'Emile'.

1780 Robert Raikes opened the first Sunday schools in Gloucester.  The movement spread and provided some sort of rudimentary education for working class children.

1800 Only 1 child in 30 had a proper education.  Some children attended a dame school but these were often inadequate.  A small minority attended grammar and public schools. There was virtually no educational provision for girls.

1803 Joseph Lancaster wrote a book called 'Improvements in Education' in which he proposed that a cheap system of education could be provided for all children.  He suggested a scheme using monitors to teach small groups within a large class which the teacher would oversee.

1808 The British and Foreign Schools Society was formed and schools which it set up were called 'British Schools' and taught non-denominational religion.

1811 The Church of England set up 'National Schools' at which the religion of the established church was taught.

1816 Robert Owen opened his progressive infant school at New Lanark.

1839 The government set up the Committee of the Privy Council for Education which super vised the paying out of new grants to schools and appointed inspectors for schools ac cepting public aid.  Extra grants were given to schools which paid and trained pupil teachers.

1860 The Revised Code was introduced to control the payment of grants to schools.  It tried to raise standards through the system of payment by results.  Grants were made to schools on the basis of regular attendance and success in examination of the 3 Rs.  Such pay ments could affect the amount available for school equipment and fuel and might even affect the teacher's salary.

1870 W.E.Forster's Education Act gave school boards power to make education compulsory in their area if they wished to do so.  Schools which they set up were called 'Board Schools' and religious teaching in them was to be non-denominational.

1874 The Factory act raised to 10 the age at which a child could be employed in a factory which implies compulsory schooling up to that age.  However, this was difficult to en force especially in rural areas.

1876 and 1880   Further acts together made elementary education compulsory all over Eng land until the age of 13 although children over the age of 10 could leave if they had passed the Standard V exam.

1891 Education was made free and fees were abolished.

1897 Abolition of the Revised Code which was said to put too much pressureon both pupils and teachers and to encourage mechanical learning.

1899 The school leaving age was raised to 12.

1902-3 The school boards were abolished and replaced by new and larger education authori ties based on the county and the county borough councils.  'Board schools' became known as 'Council Schools'.  The new authorities were to be responsible for the develop ment of secondary education and Church of England 'National Schools' were to be helped by money from the rates.

*(For a full chronological outline of educational development in England and Wales see Chapter 10 of M. Hyndman's book, listed in the bibliography.)*

## APPENDIX II: MAJOR EVENTS (to put on a class time line).

| 1810 | The Kennet and Avon Canal was completed |
|------|------------------------------------------|
| 1819 | Princess Victoria was born. |
| 1825 | Stockton and Darlington Railway opened |
| 1829 | Stephenson's 'Rocket' invented. |
| 1834 | Poor Law Amendment Act |
| 1837 | Queen Victoria came to the throne |
| 1840 | Queen Victoria married Prince Albert |
|      | The Penny Post was introduced |
| 1841 | The Prince of Wales was born |
| 1842 | Female and child labour was abolished in the mines |
| 1845 | Irish potato famine |
| 1846 | The sewing machine was introduced into England |
| 1847 | Chloroform introduced |
| 1848 | First Public Health Act |
| 1851 | The Great Exhibition |
| 1854 | The Crimean War (Florence Nightingale) |
| 1857 | Indian Mutiny |
| 1858 | Huge crinolines were in fashion |
|      | Darwin's Theory of Evolution |
| 1861 | American Civil War |
|      | Prince Albert died |
| 1867 | Antiseptic methods of surgery introduced by Lister |
| 1871 | The Queen opened the Albert Hall |
| 1875 | Public Health Act |
| 1876 | The Queen made Empress of India |
| 1878 | Electric light adopted in public buildings. |
| 1880 | Boer war |
| 1887 | Queen Victoria's Golden Jubilee |
| 1888 | Local Government Act - County councils formed |
| 1890 | First motor car invented |
| 1896 | Wireless telegraphy invented |
| 1901 | Death of Queen Victoria |

## APPENDIX III: VICTORIAN CHILDREN'S NAMES

### Boys

| | | 
|---|---|
| Albert | Isaac |
| Alfred | Jacob |
| Arthur | Joseph |
| Benjamin | Joshua |
| Charles | Leonard |
| Edward | Nathaniel |
| Ernest | Septimus |
| Frederick | Silas |
| George | Simeon |
| Gilbert | Thomas |
| Harold | Walter |
| Henry | William |

### Girls

| | |
|---|---|
| Ada | Hannah |
| Alice | Harriet |
| Annie | Hope |
| Beatrice | Jemima |
| Bessie | Jessica |
| Charlotte | Lavinia |
| Eliza | Louisa |
| Ellen | Martha |
| Esther | Mercy |
| Faith | Patience |
| Fanny | Violet |
| Georgina | Zillah |

## APPENDIX IV:  FOLLOW-UP WORK

### Discussion

How do the classroom and artefacts compare with those in your own school?  Consider similarities and differences.

How do the lessons and activities compare with present day ones?

Why were teachers so strict and what does this tell us about social attitudes?

What were the aims of the 19th century school?  Are they still the same?

Do you think it is a good idea to move children up from one standard to the next solely because of academic ability?  How does your own school deal with children of different abilities?

Do children have too much freedom in the classroom nowadays?

Would children prefer to have been at school in Victorian times?  Points that might emerge in discussion  -  lessons were boring; there was too much sitting still and listening; learning e.g. by rote was mechanical and children were not encouraged to think or to use their own ideas or their imagination.

### Art and Craft

The purpose of these is to show how Victorian children were able to amuse themselves, how much time some of the richer children had to spend on such tasks and to encourage concentration and attention to detail.

    Card dolls with cut out paper clothes
    Gift containers
    Greetings cards using lace and 'scraps' or pictures from wrapping paper
    Jumping jack
    Marbling (kits from Dryads)
    Model theatre from cut-out book (Pollock)
    Model shops using plasticine or clay
    Optical illusion toys e.g. thaumatrope etc. (book available from Tridias)
    Patchwork
    Peg dolls
    Pin cushions
    Pin prick pictures
    Rag dolls
    Quilling (kits from Dryads)
    Shell scrap book
    Silhouettes
    Stencilling

*(Details of these or similar activities to be found in 'A Child's Book of Victorian Crafts' available from Sevington School - see under* **Suppliers**.*)*

### Cooking

| | |
|---|---|
| Gingerbread men | Soup |
| Gruel | Silver & gold cakes (Queen Victoria's favourites) |
| Lemon barley water | Stained glass windows |
| Real lemonade | Strawberry cordial |
| Pease pudding | Sugar mice |

*(All these recipes can be found in 'A Child's Victorian Cookery Book', available from Sevington School - see under* **Suppliers**.*)*

## Games and Rhymes

Hopscotch
Five stones
Skipping rhymes e.g.    'Up and down the ladder wall
Ha'penny loaf to feed us all;
A bit for you and a bit for me
And a bit for Punch and Judy.
(Sometimes skipping ropes had bells attached to the wooden handles).
Marbles
Nursery rhymes
Singing games such as 'Oranges and Lemons', 'Here we go round the mulberry bush' and 'The farmer's in his den'.

Keep the downstrokes straight and uniform : let the turns be round but not flat.

First go over the faint letters, then try on your own.

Least | said, | soonest | mended.

Little | wealth, | little | care.

Too many cooks spoil the broth.

Time and tide wait for no man.

## APPENDIX VI:  BIBLIOGRAPHY

### Non-fiction

| | | |
|---|---|---|
| Allen. E. | Victorian children | (A & C Black) |
| Clarke. A. | Finding out about - Victorian Schools | (Batsford) |
| Davies. P. | School Days | (Macdonald) |
| Eddershaw. D. | Period Classroom Re-creations | |
| | - Article in *Jem* 11, 1990 | (Group for Education in Museums) |
| Garlick. A.H. | A New Manual of Method. pub.1901 | (Longmans, Green & Co) |

(This is invaluable for anyone with a serious interest in Victorian Education)

| | | |
|---|---|---|
| Horn. P | The Victorian and Edwardian Schoolchild | (Alan Sutton) |
| Hyndman. M. | Schools and Schooling in England and Wales | (Harper and Row) |
| Marshall.P. | School days: a history in photographs | (Macdonald) |
| Martin. C. | Schools in history | (Wayland) |
| Morgan.J. | Great Grandma's Schooldays-Time Detectives | (Macmillan) |
| Opie. O & P. | Children's Games in Street and Playground | (O U P) |
| Purkis. S. | At School in 1900 | (Longman) |
| Purkis. S. | Exploring Schools | (Wayland) |
| Ross. A. | Going to School | (A & C Black) |
| Speed.P.E. | Learning and teaching in Victorian Times | (Longman) |
| Stoppleman.M. | School Day (Turn of the Century) | (A & C Black) |
| Thompson. F. | Lark Rise to Candleford (semi-biographical) | (Penguin) |
| Vince. J. | The Village School   (Sorbus Publications) | Available from Sevington School |
| Wardle. D. | Popular Education 1780-1975 | (C U P) |
| Wyand. J. | Village schools - A Future for the Past? | (Evans Bros.) |

(Present day photographs of old schools)

### Fiction

| | | |
|---|---|---|
| Bronte. C. | Jane Eyre  (Penguin) | |
| Dickens. C. | Nicholas Nickleby | (Penguin) |
| Hughes. T. | Tom Brown's Schooldays | (Puffin) |

## APPENDIX VII:  VICTORIAN SCHOOLS, SCHOOL MUSEUMS AND MUSEUMS OF CHILDHOOD

Ancrum Road Primary School, Ancrum Road, Dundee DD2 2XX

Angus Folk Museum, Kirkwynd, Glamis, Forfar, Angus DD8 1RT

Bethnal Green Museum of Childhood, Cambridge Heath Rd, London E2 9PA

Bishop Hooper's Schoolroom, The Folk Museum, 99-103 Westgate St, Gloucester

The Black Country Museum Trust Ltd, Tipton Road, Dudley, W. Midlands DY1 4SQ

Board School Room, The Industrial Museum, Moorside Rd, Eccleshill, Bradford BD2 3HP

British Schools Museum c/o N. Herts Museum Service, Hitchin SG5 1EQ

East Anglian Rural Life Museum, Abbot's Hall, Stowmarket IP14 1DL

Fringford Old School, c/o Fletcher's House, Woodstock, Oxon OX7 1SN

Hartlebury Castle Schoolroom, Hartlebury, Kidderminster DY11 7XZ

Herdings School Living History Centre, Norton Ave, Sheffield S14 1SL

Ironbridge Museum Victorian Schoolroom, Telford, Shropshire TF8 7AW

Judge's Lodgings Museum of Childhood, Lancaster LA1 1YS

Katesgrove Schoolroom, Katesgrove Primary School, Dorothy St, Reading RG1 2NL

Leeds Industrial Museum, Armley Mill, Canal Road, Leed LS12 2QF

London Street Primary School, East London Street, Edinburgh EH7 4BW

Macclesfield Heritage Centre, Roe Street, Macclesfield, SK11 6UT

Museum of Childhood, 42, High Street, Edinburgh EH7 4BW

Museum of the History of Education, Room 14, Parkinson Court,
    The University, Leeds LS2 9JT
Museum of Labour History, Islington, Merseyside L3 8EE
New Lanark Conservation Trust, New Lanark Mills, Lanark ML11 9DB
North of England Open Air Museum, Beamish, Co. Durham, DH9 ORG
Ragged School Museum Trust, 46-48, Copperfield Rd, London E3 4RR
St. Fagan's Welsh Folk Museum, near Cardiff, South Glamorgan, Wales CF5 6XB
Scotland Street School Museum, 225, Scotland Street, Glasgow G5 8QB
Sevington School, Sevington, Chippenham, Wilts SN14 7LD
Staffordshire County Museums Service, Shugborough Hall, Shugborough, Staffs
Stibbington Board School, Great Northern Rd, Stibbington, Peterborough PE8 6PL
Sudbury Hall Museum of Childhood, Sudbury, Derby DE6 5HT
Tudor House Museum, Friar Street, Worcester WR1 2NA
Ulster Folk Park, Camphill, Castletown, Omagh, County Tyrone BT78 5QY
Ulster Folk and Transport Museum, Cultra Mnor, Holywood, Co.Down BT18 0EU
Warwickshire Museums Service, St, John's House Museum, Warwick CV34 4QU
Weald and Downland Museum, Singleton, near Chichester, W. Sussex PO18 OEU
Wigan Pier Heritage Centre, Wigan WN3 4EU

*(For more details consult a Gazeteer of Period Classrooms appended to David Eddershaw's article - see under **Bibliography**).*

## APPENDIX VIII: SUPPLIERS

1. **Copybooks**
   Sevington School, Sevington, Chippenham, Wilts. SN14 7LD
   (Send for mail order list and form)
2. **Books**
   'A Visit to Queen Victoria' - a reproduction story book.
   'The New Reading Easy or Child's First Book' - reproduction copy.
   'The Historical House that Jack Built' - reproduction copy.
   'A Child's Victorian Cookery Book' - a modern collection.
   'A Child's Book of Victorian Crafts'- a modern collection.
   All from Sevington School, Sevington, Chippenham, Wilts. SN14 7LD.
3. **Resource material about education and childhood**
   Many of museums listed above, especially
   The Museum of Childhood, Bethnal Green, Cambridge Heath Rd, London.
   The Museum of Childhood, 42, High Street, Edinburgh EH1 1TG.
4. **Slates and slate pencils**
   Katesgrove Schoolroom, Katesgrove Primary School, Dorothy Street, Reading,
   Berks. RG1 2NL
   Sevington School (as above).
5. **Dip-in pens**
   Sevington School (as above).
6. **Traditional toys**
   Katesgrove Schoolroom (as above).
   Sevington School (as above).
7. **Traditional toys and toy-making workshops**
   Cyril Hobbins is an ex-woodwork teacher who runs very reasonably priced workshops
   for teachers or pupils (you keep the toys you have made).
   Little Wood Studio 'Arnside', 11, Castle Road, Kenilworth, Warks. CV8 1NG.
   (Send for mail order list).